I0096347

The Spirit is in the Room

ANGELA SARAFIN, M.A., LMFT

THE SPIRIT
IS IN THE
ROOM

CHRISTIANITY & CREATIVITY IN EMDR THERAPY

Except where noted otherwise, scripture quotations are from the ESV® Bible (The Holy Bible, English Standard Version®), © 2001 by Crossway, a publishing ministry of Good News Publishers. Used by permission. All rights reserved. The ESV text may not be quoted in any publication made available to the public by a Creative Commons license. The ESV may not be translated in whole or in part into any other language.

Scripture quotations marked (CEV) are from the Contemporary English Version Copyright © 1991, 1992, 1995 by American Bible Society. Used by Permission.

Scripture quotations marked (MSG) are taken from The Message, copyright © 1993, 2002, 2018 by Eugene H. Peterson. Used by permission of NavPress. All rights reserved. Represented by Tyndale House Publishers.

Cover design by #optimalgraphics
Illustrations by the author, Angela Sarafin

The Spirit is in the Room: Christianity and Creativity in EMDR Therapy
Copyright @2025 by Angela Sarafin
Published by Platypus Publishing

Library of Congress Cataloging Data
The Spirit is in the Room: Christianity and Creativity in EMDR Therapy / Angela Sarafin
ISBN: 978-1-965016-75-6
Trauma Psychology/Spiritually Integrated Psychotherapy/Christian Counseling

Printed in The United States of America

DEDICATION

This book is dedicated to the many clients who
gave me the honor of walking with them through
their healing journey.

CONTENTS

Acknowledgements...ix

Introduction xiii

1. THE PREDICTION GENERATOR.....................................1
2. THE MEANDERING PATH...5
3. THE PURSUIT OF BEING TRANSFORMED.....................19
4. MIX AND MATCH..25
5. MAKING SENSE OF THE CHAOS.....................................35
6. PREPARATION IS THE WORK...53
7. SETTING THE STAGE..73
8. ASSESSING THE TARGET..85
9. DOING EMDR...97
10. INSTALLING THE GOOD..123
11. LEAVING THE PAIN IN THE PAST................................131
12. BEAUTY FROM ASHES...137
13. BE STRONG AND COURAGEOUS...................................145

BONUS CHAPTERS
STIRRING CREATIVITY...151
HELP FOR THERAPISTS..159

EMDR PHASES DIAGRAM..169
STAGES OF CHANGE DIAGRAM...170

SUGGESTED RESOURCES..171
GLOSSARY...175

ACKNOWLEDGEMENTS

God provided some really special people to influence, challenge, and encourage me in my spiritual and professional journey.

Patti Marik, thank you for loving me when I was unlovable and teaching me how to be a female entrepreneur.

Debbie Hampton, thank you for bringing me into the fold as "the baby" in the Journey to Joy women's group. The women there taught me so much about being a woman of God.

Amy Dunniway, thank you for showing me what it means to be bold in the faith.

Thank you to the sisters of my heart, Lora Doremus, Jenny Verghese, and Sonja Galliani. We had such a sweet season of praying together and "getting real." I will treasure that always.

Erin Brindle, thank you for being adventurous and attending that first EMDR training with me in Virginia Beach. You inspire me to be more creative both personally and professionally.

Deborah Bumbaugh, you always make me feel "delighted in." You have such a gift for radiating God's love and encouragement.

Cyndi Wagner, you inspire me to be more vocal about giving God the glory. I have appreciated your spontaneous curbside prayers when we are out walking in the city.

Zack and Autumn Randles, thank you for bringing Mike and me into your circle. I deeply appreciate your encouragement and support.

Jan Walker, thank you for challenging me to be nice to myself and for being a cheerleader for this book.

Chad, you are the best brother. I couldn't have custom ordered anyone better. Thank you for being my best friend through all the transitions of our childhood. Thanks for taking the leap first in so many situations and showing me what was possible.

Dad, thank you for encouraging me to think both logically and creatively and helping me at various stages of business ownership.

Mom, thank you for pursuing me and figuring out that going for a walk helped me talk when I was upset. I think you were onto something even before Francine Shapiro.

I also want to thank Delee D'Arcy, Deborah Bumbaugh, and Autumn Randles for being first readers of my first version and providing motivation to keep refining the narrative.

It's hard to move from storyteller to editor, so thank you to my volunteer editors for helping me make that shift. Special thanks to Cathy Landry for the critical but constructive editing feedback on my very rough first draft and to Laura Niver, who caught all my grammar and punctuation issues in the last draft.

I really could not have made it through the editing process without my husband, Michael. Thank you for reading, and re-reading, and reading yet again. Your calm, methodical way helps steady my creative whirlwind tendencies. Thank you for cheering me on and giving me space to try new things, even though they are often not risks you would choose.

INTRODUCTION

When I was in my 20s, I experienced panic attacks just before a few critical decision points in life. Similar to touching a hot stove, my body pulled away from the pain before I was consciously aware of the burn. Once I learned to recognize that warning system, I got more curious about what felt ill-fitting and what dreams were emerging. My last panic attack occurred in the summer of 2002 while I was working at a major oil company in Houston, TX. After several months of self-reflection (and counseling), I realized that my job felt pointless because it was not really improving people's lives. That realization led me to pursue a Master's degree in Marriage and Family Therapy. I was ready to leave immediately, but my husband asked me to keep my job for another year. I unhappily agreed to that plan. I had no idea how to balance the demands of that job and keep up with homework assignments.

It was a shock when the company offered a voluntary layoff plan just a few weeks after I enrolled in school. The layoff was a tremendous gift from God. Not only was I freed from a suffocating job, but I also started my graduate degree debt-free.

In addition to the lump sum payment, the severance package included free enrollment in an outplacement program. Most of the offerings were simple job search and resume writing support, but one option captured my attention, a five-day entrepreneurship workshop. As the instructor led us through imaginative activities I happily played with colored markers and let my imagination run wild. One activity involved imagining life from the point of unemployment forward through death. That vast blank space on the page was daunting. I remember feeling reluctant to write any future goals because I was afraid of failing. The instructor challenged me to consider the activity as a space for dreams rather than goals to achieve. I found that life map recently and was surprised to find "write a book" clearly written for this phase of my life. Isn't it funny how we sometimes know before we know?

The idea for "The Spirit is in the Room" came to me early in the morning on February 26, 2024. I know this only because I wrote the idea in my journal. This book is an answer to prayer. The previous day, Waterfront Church DC pastor Zack Randles said, "When you feel uneasy about something, visit the monuments." This has a dual meaning for us here in Washington, DC, because the city is full of physical monuments and points of interest to remind people of specific events, people, and turning points in the life of the city and the United States. But the sermon also referred to spiritual monuments.

It is not unusual for me to feel amazed at Zack's ability to recall his spiritual monuments and tell stories from his life as illustrations of God's presence, provision, and character. As I listened to that sermon, none of my own stories came to mind. I felt an odd sense of alarm, so I asked God to show me my spiritual monuments.

I remember feeling sad as I spoke that prayer. Some people easily recall memories by category, such as "my favorite vacation" or "the best book I've read." My brain does not work well that way. I often need spatial cues to spark my memory. For example, when I was in college, I hand wrote my notes, and when I needed to recall something, the first thing I would remember was where I wrote the concept on my paper - upper left, lower right, in the margin, circled in yellow, etc. If you ask me if I have seen a particular movie (apart from my favorites that I have watched a dozen times), I am very likely to give you a blank stare and say, "I'm not sure." If you provide a little bit about the storyline and which actors were in the movie, I will probably tell you, "That sounds familiar." However, if my husband was with me when I saw the movie, he could tell you when we saw it, where we saw it, and who else went with us. That spatial context information eventually helps me recall something specific from the movie. I also tend to remember isolated scenes but not the full arc of the story. It's very annoying at times, but it does allow me to enjoy rewatching TV shows and movies because I have a general sense of "Oh, I liked that." So I go in with positive expectations but often feel like I'm watching the movie for the first time again.

Why am I telling you this? Because I often think that God created me with a brain built for client confidentiality. Although I have heard many stories from clients, those stories are not easy for me to recall. The snapshots in this book, vignettes as we call them in the therapy world, are moments that God specifically brought back to my conscious mind to help, encourage, and illustrate. Although all vignettes are from real client cases, names and identifying details were changed to protect confidentiality.

If you are a therapist like me, at one point, you believed in Eye-Movement Desensitization and Reprocessing therapy (EMDR) enough that you spent thousands of dollars to go through Basic Training. You may have even spent thousands more on individual and group consultations to get certified. Yet, you might still feel hesitant to use EMDR with your clients. If so, I hope that this book will help you find a path forward to use EMDR in a way that fits with your counseling style and your clients' needs. I see EMDR as an effective tool for many, but I also believe other great tools exist. I encourage you to ask God for wisdom to determine which modalities best serve your clients.

If you are a client undergoing EMDR, I hope these stories from the therapy room will clarify the EMDR process and illustrate how faith and creativity fit into the healing process.

If you are on the periphery, perhaps considering EMDR therapy or in a position to refer others to counseling, I hope that this book will spark your imagination and inspire healing conversations. There are many different approaches to counseling and it is impossible to explain them all in one book. This book includes several different methods and I encourage you to note what resonates most as you think about the challenges at the top of your mind for you and those who confide in you.

This book is primarily a written account of the perspectives I often share with other therapists, including ideas and techniques I pieced together over the years to inspire creativity in the counseling room and encourage the integration of intuition and formal process. I firmly believe that counseling works best when there is co-creation, so I encourage the therapist and the motivated client to take what feels useful and relevant from this book. I also (not-so-secretly) hope that you will consider using EMDR. A few extra resources are included at the end of the book to help you access your creativity. I also included a quick reference section for EMDR therapists.

Except as otherwise noted, all scripture references come from The Holy Bible, English Standard Version.

One final note: I have attended many training classes and read multiple books on EMDR and trauma work. The EMDR standard protocol is the work of Francine Shapiro, who created EMDR. I have done my best to give credit where credit is due for other ideas and techniques. I learned some techniques from multiple sources and am uncertain who to credit as originators/inventors.

If you notice any egregious omissions, please feel free to contact me. It is not my intention to steal work but to show some ways that a broad collection of ideas and frameworks can work together synergistically.

So, let's dive in.

CHAPTER ONE

THE PREDICTION GENERATOR

We often go about our daily lives in a trance, operating off what we expect to happen rather than what is happening. How often do you consciously anticipate the step off of a curb and consider how to adjust your gait in the following moment? I know I usually don't consciously think about it unless I step off a curb that is shorter or taller than I expected. Without conscious effort, we constantly predict what will happen next. A team at the University of Sussex in the United Kingdom has been researching consciousness and have come to the conclusion that the mind is a prediction machine that constantly runs simulations based on models of ourselves and the world around us, setting up our expectations.

We expect a pen to make a mark on a page, so we start writing, predicting that the pen will work. However, when our prediction is proven wrong, we are abruptly jolted back into the present moment. There is momentary confusion or consternation before the brain begins predicting what will solve the problem. We shake the pen, scribble on the back of the page, lick the tip, maybe open the pen to see if any ink is still visible in the barrel, etc. A similar process occurs for nearly every little aspect of life.

The mind's simulations are used to predict how to survive and adapt in various imagined situations. Built into the simulation process is an evaluation of "the most likely scenario" which becomes our default expectation. Unlike pure mathematics based only on statistical odds, our personal "most likely scenarios" include our personal experiences and what we have determined is true for us. For example, "I'm lucky, I always get a parking spot near the store," or "If there's something that's going to go wrong, it will happen to me."

People end up in therapy when the prediction generator malfunctions – when data goes missing or when there's a short in the power supply. It feels uncomfortable, sometimes even intolerable, when we can't predict what is next or understand why our prediction was wrong. We might experience a failed prediction when we give someone a gift. We wait with excitement, expecting wonder or laughter from the other person. If we receive a fake smile and a vague thank you, we feel confused about why the other person is not pleased with the gift. Similarly, when we are living in the 'not yet' phase for longer than expected - not yet married, not yet promoted, not yet a parent, not yet healed, etc. - we feel restless and uncomfortable and start to wonder why God is not providing as we expected. It's just in our nature to be confused by failed predictions.

Another primary focus of our minds is to make meaning. Interpreting the meaning or purpose of an experience helps fuel the prediction generator. The meanings we create about specific events and patterns either narrow or expand our expectations of safety and danger. For example, the thought "I cannot trust my instincts" increases the sense of danger and leads to hyper-vigilance – constantly scanning for threats, leading to exhaustion. Conversely, the thought "Nothing is working" also increases the sense of danger, but with a different result. Instead of scanning for danger, our minds search for an escape route, fueling hopelessness as time goes on without relief or resolution.

People have a hard time accepting alternate perspectives.

The challenge in therapy is that even if we identify the thought fueling the prediction generator's endless loop, people have a hard time accepting alternate perspectives. I include myself in that observation. After engaging in therapy for several years, I decided to hire a different therapist because the first therapist struggled to help me recalibrate my prediction generator. Our last few sessions were particularly challenging for both of us; my mind instantly rejected every alternative she offered. Rather than co-creating viable options, we reached a stalemate, leaving me feeling misunderstood and her … well, I can only speculate. For some reason, God's spirit of creativity was missing from the process.

I don't share this story to discredit my previous therapist; she was a supportive presence during an extended waiting phase in my life. However, my prediction generator did not get the jolt it needed until I found a therapist who invited the Holy Spirit's creative energy into our sessions. Interestingly, she is also an EMDR therapist.

As you read through this story, I encourage you to keep in mind how your prediction generator is working. Is that creativity moving you toward your goals, or is it keeping you stuck in fear or pessimism? What is it telling you about how to find success and satisfaction personally and professionally? And is that grounded in the truth?

CHAPTER TWO

THE MEANDERING PATH

Therapy is my second career. I took a meandering path through engineering and criminal justice before finally graduating with a Bachelor's degree in computer science. I also enjoy playing music, acting in plays, and creating art. Oh, and did I mention that I love puzzles? To say that I have an eclectic set of skills and interests would be putting it mildly. Some people are confused by my switch from computer science to counseling. On the surface, the two fields seem entirely unrelated.

Unlike many computer scientists, computer programming was boring to me. However, I enjoyed figuring out what the client wanted and needed and determining what was technologically feasible. The thrill of finding a creative answer to a complex problem unifies these seemingly opposite career fields (at least from my perspective). Give me variety, new puzzles, and a chance to use my imagination, and I feel right in my element. My husband pointed out that even writing this book has been a puzzle-solving experience for me.

When I decided to switch careers from Computer Science, several different "helping professional" degree plans were available at the local universities. I chose to study Marriage and Family Therapy because working with people in the context of their relationships makes sense to me intuitively. Over the first few years of my counseling career, I saw a few of my colleagues incorporate their Christian beliefs into their counseling. I liked the idea of bringing spiritual faith into my work but lacked confidence in my Bible knowledge. I spent a few years gathering knowledge through self-paced theological studies and Biblical counseling conferences.

I encountered a few people who challenged my decision to work as a licensed professional instead of working within a church environment. That criticism caused me to pause and question my path, but God reminded me that a lot of people have no connection to a church. Interestingly, Christian clients found their way to my practice even before I advertised myself as a faith-based counselor.

Overall, the work was going well. The business grew, and I started training other therapists. However, as I approached the "expert" phase of my career (that 10,000-hour mark where the task becomes second nature), I encountered two particular client situations that seemed resistant to all my therapeutic interventions. I will refer to these clients as "Claire" and "Tasha." I learned a lot about trauma responses from those ladies and one unfortunate opossum.

My husband and I had a squirrel problem when we lived in Houston. Squirrels chewed through the siding of our house and made nests in the attic and walls. My husband initiated a squirrel hunting campaign to trap and remove squirrels from our property. On one occasion, we had an unexpected guest in one of the traps. An opossum had squeezed himself into the trap. I don't think he could even turn around inside of it. The opossum started hissing at us as we approached the trap. I was scared at first and kept my distance from the trap. In contrast, my husband moved toward the trap with interest and told me, "He's a harmless bug-eating critter. He's just scared." That opossum knew it was trapped and its defense mechanisms were in full effect, but he needed someone brave enough to approach and set him free.

That opossum reminded me of Claire. She knew her behavior patterns were problematic, but she was very defensive and reluctant to accept help. Claire told me she was Jewish, so I did my best to utilize her faith beliefs to help her find a sense of grounding. She continued meeting with me for the better part of 2 years. Sometimes, the therapy seemed to help, but periodically, she turned hostile and accused me of being incompetent. When Claire accused me of not helping, I tried to refer her to an intensive outpatient program so she could keep her job and have more consistent counseling support, but she always refused. I kept seeing her because I did not want to fail. In many frustrating moments, I desperately wanted to get off that merry-go-round of emotional manipulation. I could not figure out how to safely exit the situation. Although I had provided her with several other counseling options, I was afraid to end the relationship because inciting her hostility meant jeopardizing my therapy license.

One day, that hostility showed up anyway. Claire decided that I was the enemy because I am a Christian, and she fired me as her therapist. Our first meeting occurred in a church building and we discussed the fact that I attended that church. I did not hide my faith from her. I tell you this story to remind you that, as Christians, we are going to be rejected sometimes, even by the people who are intrigued at the beginning. It is also helpful to remember that, sometimes, the familiarity of the current life (even if painful) will overpower a person's desire to change. While many would consider my time with Claire a failure, I know that ultimately, God is the one who empowers me and who empowers a person's willingness and ability to have hope and be transformed.

That dynamic reminds me of the Israelites sending twelve spies to explore the promised land (Numbers chapter 13). Despite of coming back with an abundance of grapes, evidence of what was good about the land, most of the spies were more fearful than hopeful. Their prediction generators said, "If we try to occupy the land, we will die. The people there are too big and too numerous for us to defeat." Only Joshua and Caleb remained excited and hopeful because they were confident in God's ability and willingness to help them prevail against seemingly unbeatable odds.

I can take heart regarding Claire's situation because the outcome is in God's hands. I do my best, and God fills the gap, just as he does for all Christ-followers. I never saw Claire again, but I still pray that God will give her the courage she needs to trust Him and live a fruitful life.

God empowers a person's willingness and ability to change.

The second challenging client was "Tasha." Even now, when I learn about a new trauma treatment technique, I think about Tasha. She had a pretty rough childhood with some abuse and a lot of neglect. During the time she was in my care, Tasha went through the dismantling of her "nice life" when her husband abandoned her and took the kids. I knew that God wanted to heal her emotional wounds, and I knew that there must be a way to help her recover from this repeating cycle of abuse, neglect, and abandonment. Sadly, the core of her pain persisted despite the strength of our rapport and all my therapeutic efforts. This therapeutic plateau inspired me to look for other therapeutic interventions beyond my Family Therapy training.

My first foray into non-traditional trauma treatment was the Emotional Freedom Technique (EFT) developed by Gary Craig. Some of my clients referred to EFT as "that tapping thing." In EFT, the therapist and client work together to identify something that the client feels unable to handle. The goal is to reduce negative thoughts and emotions related to that topic and thus remove barriers to change. Then, the therapist leads the client through a sequence of tapping specific points on the face, torso, and hands while saying a phrase such as "Even though I believe I have no self-control, I deeply and completely love myself." The underlined words can be replaced with whatever is relevant for the client, such as "I'm craving a cigarette" or "I can't catch a break."

I used EFT with Tasha. The technique was somewhat helpful, and Tasha experienced some symptom relief. However, when I looked at the efficacy across multiple client cases, EFT provided short-term symptom relief, but I did not see lasting change.

There is also a "weird" factor to the technique that made it a hard sell with some clients. I used EFT during an in-school workshop where I taught stress reduction for teens with test anxiety. As I was leading them through the tapping technique, one kid said, "I feel like I'm trying to pound calm into my face." The workshop went downhill from there. Eventually, I abandoned EFT tapping and went in search of other options.

Around 2007, I met several therapists who used EMDR. It sounded intriguing, but I was uncertain whether to trust their enthusiasm for the technique. My counseling professors had talked about EMDR as if it was a gimmick rather than a real therapeutic technique.

Fast forward to today, EMDR has existed for more than 30 years and has a proven track record for helping resolve post-traumatic symptoms by reducing emotional reactivity and bringing the mind and body into agreement that the past event is not happening now. As neurobiology has advanced and provided more insight into how trauma impacts the brain and research has been done on various treatment modalities, EMDR has become more mainstream within the counseling community. The name, if not the mechanics, is also more familiar to the general public after several celebrities spoke openly in recent years about how EMDR helped them.

EMDR brings the mind and body into agreement that the past event is not happening now.

The most "famous" aspect of EMDR is the eye-movements. This form of bilateral stimulation (BLS) alternates visual focus or stimulation from one side of the body to the other. In the context of memory processing, BLS is also called dual-awareness stimulation (DAS). EMDR founder Francine Shapiro first discovered the healing power of BLS when she was walking (a bilateral movement) and moving her eyes from one side of the path to the other while thinking about a troubling situation. By the end of the walk, she realized she felt much differently about the situation. She took that discovery into the counseling room, where it ultimately evolved into EMDR therapy.

Years after EMDR had taken off as a therapeutic method, other researchers found that other forms of bilateral movement (walking, tactile stimuli, bilateral sound) all have impacts on the brain's memory networks. Shapiro later concluded that the key to memory desensitization may be the dual awareness rather than eye-movements specifically. I think God was very creative in offering such a wide range of healing aids within the normal range of how we use our bodies. EMDR simply uses those actions in a more focused and deliberate fashion.

I wanted to learn EMDR while working with Tasha, but the training course fee was well beyond my means at that time. When I talked with a few colleagues about other techniques for complex trauma cases, several suggested hypnosis. I had some hesitations about hypnosis because it always seemed a bit terrifying to let someone else muck around with my thoughts when they could cause me to forget that it had happened. Even so, I needed some continuing education credits in order to renew my therapy license, so I signed up for a hypnosis training weekend.

The class was valuable in that it completely reinforced my fear of hypnosis. Not to sound overly religious, but it felt like the trainer had a demonic force attached to him. It was an exceedingly unsafe emotional experience for me to even be in the same room with him, and I vowed I would never intentionally put a client into a situation where they were completely "at my mercy" and unable to stop, pause, or redirect the process. Is hypnosis evil? I don't know, but it was clear that it was not spiritually healthy for me to pursue.

EMDR ≠ hypnosis

People often confuse EMDR with hypnosis because movies have historically shown the hypnotist swinging a watch or other object in front of the client, using eye-movements and a specific vocal pattern to lull the client into a hypnotic state. The difference between EMDR and hypnosis is who is in charge, the nature of the altered state, and the duration of that state. In hypnosis, the hypnotist is in charge. The client does not direct their attention to the "problem" until they are in the hypnotic state. Hypnosis is immersive, lasting for 30 to 60 minutes at a time. Depending on the purpose of the hypnosis, the hypnotist may insert a post-hypnotic suggestion designed to direct the client's future actions. In EMDR, the starting point and goal of the process are determined and agreed to by the client in advance of any BLS.

While a hypnotized client stays in a particular memory or suggested place for a prolonged amount of time, in EMDR, the goal is to have dual awareness, staying aware of where they are bodily (specifically that they are in a safe place) while thinking about a disturbing memory. EMDR keeps these exposures short, usually only about 30 seconds, to allow the client to process the memory without getting pulled into re-experiencing the full effects. When done well, EMDR provides a level of safety for the client, even when experiencing unpleasant emotions or body sensations. Any suggestions from the therapist occur when the client is not engaged in BLS. The client has the choice to entertain or dismiss the therapist's comments. I sometimes let BLS go beyond 30 seconds to allow the client to visualize something helpful but not to go digging around in distressing memories.

After that hypnosis training weekend, I continued to explore avenues for EMDR training and eventually found an organization called The Green Cross Academy of Traumatology that offered one weekend of EMDR training at a very affordable price. I decided to attend that training to confirm that I liked EMDR well enough to invest in the complete training. I was drawn to this specific training class because a Christian university hosted it. I trusted that if the course had a spiritual component, the facilitators would call on Jesus and not some other unnamed spirit. That weekend confirmed my interest in adding EMDR to my counseling practice.

Done well, EMDR provides safety to help clients cope with unpleasant feelings.

The Basic Training is considered the minimal level of education to use EMDR competently with clients. The process requires four days of training classes plus ten hours of case consultation. The course is usually taught over two separate weekends, about a month apart, so the trainee can practice with clients and bring questions to the second training session. Basic Training covers a process called The Standard Protocol which involves eight phases. The course also requires trainees to practice the technique with each other, taking turns acting as clients or EMDR therapists. There were usually two practice sessions each day. There is a lot packed into those four class days.

Being the client in a training class requires a lot of vulnerability. Most service professions require this type of peer practice. I remember a chiropractor telling me horror stories about receiving adjustments from some of his peers during the in-school practicum. His stories made me cringe. It would take a lot of courage for me to let a novice manipulate my spine. For some people, trusting someone with their emotional pain requires great courage, and we do well to remember that.

Because of the certification rules at the time, I had to repeat the first weekend's classes, but this was a blessing in disguise. As the second EMDR course proceeded, my training partner was not attuned to what was happening with me when I was in the client role. Although I thought I had chosen a "small" issue in my life, it opened a big trauma hole, and I felt very agitated; my breathing became labored, and I started crying. Even though I was clearly getting emotionally dysregulated (as opposed to staying in a relatively calm learning state), my training partner just followed the script rather than pausing to check in and see how I was doing. Her dismissal of my distress destroyed my ability to trust her. I might have been scared off by that experience had I not completed prior EMDR training. On the upside, the negative training experience reinforced my commitment to protect my clients.

My negative experience made me more protective of my clients.

When I finally finished the Basic Training, I soon realized I had only just begun. It was a bit like my experience at the end of my master's degree when I realized how much more training I still needed. After completing all the Basic Training requirements, the EMDR International-al Association (EMDRIA) certification process requires an additional twenty hours of consultation plus twelve hours of education in advanced EMDR topics.

In 2017, it was more difficult to find a local EMDR consultant than it is today. After exploring my options, I joined a monthly consultation group. By this point in my career, I had worked with several supervisors and consultants, but this consulting experience was probably the most odd and awkward.

For the first year of consultation, it seemed as if the consultant did not like me, and I rarely received any encouragement or show of confidence in my clinical skills. As a consequence, I started to question my competence. I also felt somewhat discouraged and confused because there were therapists who had attended consultation groups for many years, and yet they seemed to ask basic EMDR questions. Since I rarely felt stuck in my client cases and had no burning questions to address in the group, I began to wonder if I was the incompetent one and didn't know enough to recognize it.

I have encountered other therapists in this same predicament, having their confidence undermined by fearful people around them. Perhaps this is a normal part of the growth process that we must push through. At some point, we all encounter a crossroads where we must choose whether to believe in ourselves and what the Holy Spirit is saying or let other people's fears hold us still.

CHAPTER THREE

THE PURSUIT OF BEING TRANSFORMED

Crossroads are dangerous places of opportunity. Regardless of which way you go, you still have to navigate the intersection. People often come to counseling because they feel stuck at a crossroads. They desire to change, but nothing seems to be moving or working well, or everything is changing, and they feel stuck in fear. Either way, feeling trapped is a pattern of the world that God does not want for us.

Ideally, for those of us who are followers of Jesus, when our circumstances are not changing, we are waiting patiently on God's next instruction and either growing or resting in preparation for the next phase. When everything is changing, we are in the middle of being transplanted. Sometimes, God replants us in the same place after He tills the soil; other times, we get completely relocated. The process is often disorienting, but God is simply calling us into something new. We need not fear or worry about our future. I suspect that perspective enabled the Apostle Paul to say that he had learned to be content in all circumstances (Philippians 4:11).

With God, we are never stuck; waiting is often part of His plan. Unfortunately, most of us struggle to stay rooted in this hope. Our prediction-generating minds frequently return us to states of fear and discouragement. That is a battle EMDR can help us fight.

EMDR can help us fight the internal battle between hope and fear.

Many EMDR-trained therapists struggle to incorporate the EMDR process into their client work. This is a crossroads, requiring re-imagining the therapy process with a new perspective and additional tools. It takes time to adjust the sense of self from "talk therapist" to "EMDR therapist." I was trapped at that crossroads for a while. The more I tried to ensure I was doing EMDR "the right way," the more the client sessions felt stilted and a little boring. Worse, some clients circumvented the process, telling me what they thought I wanted to hear so the process could end as quickly as possible.

In theory, incorporating EMDR into my work with clients should have become more manageable once I memorized scripts for the EMDR process. In actuality, I lost my identity for a while because fear held me captive.

Before the training, I moved through the intake and assessment process with effortless fluidity; I playfully engaged clients in imagining alternate interpretations and drew out a client's illogical beliefs until they could laugh at the absurdity. All that ease disappeared when I started using EMDR with my clients. My interactions with clients became more hesitant and awkward, and I knew the clients were beginning to think, "I'm not sure if she knows what she's doing."

Considering that I had ten years of counseling experience before starting EMDR training, it is alarming that I felt like a complete novice after the Basic Training process. Looking back, I wish the training taught both how to do the process and how to integrate EMDR into my already established and unique way of working with clients. I have encountered quite a few therapists who abandoned EMDR after the costly training investment. It makes me wonder whether there is something in the basic training program that makes us afraid to bring our unique counseling styles into the EMDR process.

I must give credit to God because at my lowest point of confidence, when I could have abandoned EMDR, I chose instead to hire a different EMDR case consultant.

The second consultant experience was better because she focused more on the mentoring relationship and less on strict adherence to the standard protocol. She gave me the gift of listening and affirming that I was "on the right track" with my case conceptualizations and intervention choices. Even when she offered corrections, she still communicated that I was doing well and that I had good instincts about what my clients needed. She also taught me creative methods to enhance clients' confidence about working on difficult memories. As a result, I felt freer to use my intuition to customize the EMDR process to suit each client's needs.

Customizing the EMDR therapy process (or altering the standard protocol) seems to be a minefield. On the one hand, numerous therapists have developed alternative protocols for special purposes such as addictions, recent events, recurring events, physical pain, etc. Many EMDRIA-approved continuing education courses teach these "advanced" protocols. In contrast, Attachment-Focused EMDR, created by Laurel Parnell, was initially on EMDRIA's approval list but was later excluded. Since I am not privy to EMDRIA's decision-making process, I felt confused and uncertain about what are or are not reasonable and credible alterations to EMDR.

Regardless of EMDRIA's stance, I appreciate Dr. Parnell's contribution to the EMDR world. During a webinar a few years ago, Dr. Parnell described her adaptations to the setup and several other aspects of the standard protocol to promote more connection between therapist and client. As I listened to her rationale for adjusting elements of the standard protocol, I felt validated because my intuition had led me to some of the same conclusions and adjustments.

Something about tapping into intuition is profoundly satisfying for me. My favorite way to play with intuition is through brainstorming projects. Since I don't have many group project opportunities at this point in life, case consultations with counseling colleagues are my primary opportunity for this type of play. A few years ago, several of my colleagues came to me (separately) with questions related to EMDR cases. Collectively, their feedback on our discussions was that I explained things in a way that made a lot of sense, and they concluded that I should become an EMDRIA consultant.

EMDRIA is the association that has the most extensive history of certifying EMDR therapists in the US, although the EMDR Global Network now offers a separate certification option. To become certified as an EMDRIA-approved consultant, one has to be a certified EMDR provider and then engage in an additional twenty hours of meetings with an EMDRIA-approved consultant as a consultant-in-training. So, I started down that path, not because I was excited about it, but because that was the obvious direction to go next. It was as if I'd been dating EMDRIA so long that we might as well get married. But like an ill-advised marriage, it was not a good fit for me, and I quit the Consultant in Training process less than a year later. I found the role irritating and restrictive and eventually realized that I did not want to be in the position of deciding whether someone had demonstrated adequate mastery of EMDR therapy.

The evaluation responsibility took all the fun out of therapeutic case consultation. Yet, I still want to help other therapists find joy and ease with EMDR therapy, and the best way I know to do that is to share my process.

The next obvious step is not necessarily the best option.

True to my personality, my therapeutic approach is eclectic, but I found a few specific frameworks that work well together. Rather than outline each aspect of my therapeutic approach separately, I decided it is more beneficial to structure the next part of the book according to the eight phases of EMDR (as explained in Francine Shapiro's book *Eye-Movement Desensitization and Reprocessing: basic principles, protocols, and procedures*). I believe this will demonstrate how different therapeutic frameworks may be integrated into each phase of EMDR.

CHAPTER FOUR

MIX
AND
MATCH

In graduate school, one of my major assignments was a paper about my theoretical framework for therapy. It was a confusing assignment because the professors suggested that being an eclectic theorist was bad, yet none of the existing theoretical frameworks captured how I saw the world. It felt like a cop-out when I wrote my paper about my eclectic (mix and match) theoretical approach. It's funny that, almost 20 years later, I am writing a book about how my theoretical approach evolved.

As mentioned earlier, my master's program was marriage and family therapy. Family therapy is fundamentally about how we operate within relational contexts or systems. Sometimes, we get to choose our roles; other times, the system selects the role for us.

One of my favorite concepts from systems theory is homeostasis, the principle that systems default to maintaining balance and resisting change. I see this even in my own story; for example, when my former therapist was providing ideas about ways I could approach my marriage differently, I kept rejecting her suggestions. Although I believe that I had good reason to reject some of the suggestions, I also know that part of me was resisting change because I was afraid of creating too much disruption in my marriage. As a cog in the machine of my marriage, I was doing a great job of maintaining homeostasis even though the stable marital situation was also maintaining a certain level of distress for me as an individual.

When I think of my resistance to change, I have more patience for my clients who are unable or unwilling to push against the status quo. It creates an interesting push-pull when we consider our minds as prediction generators trying to find the path of least pain. It's easy to get stuck when the solution for a current pain has a high potential for initiating a new pain point. It makes sense then that we need time to prepare for change.

We need time to prepare for change.

When considering why a client is stuck on a past event, I refer to the theory behind EMDR, the Adaptive Information Processing (AIP) model. AIP posits that, in most cases, our minds can distill an experience into usable (adaptive) information. Adaptive information allows us to make decisions based on past experiences, good or bad. However, some experiences are so far outside our framework for understanding the world that our brains can't make sense of the information. This confusion results in endless loops of flashbacks, nightmares, and other trauma symptoms. In my own story, this occurred when I felt abandoned by my adult friends because I had an unprocessed childhood memory. I did not realize that memory was traumatic until I noticed my brain stuck in the negative loop, "people say they like me, but they never choose me."

It's hard to make sense of events far outside our understanding of the world.

In contrast, my client Tasha's "normal" experiences for close relationships were that people were either overly attentive toward her or acted as if she did not exist. She was either the whole universe or nothing at all to people. She knew she did not like either extreme, so she married a man who seemed to exist between those two extremes. He shared some of her interests but was not "needy" or demanding, so she felt safe with him. When he decided he did not want to be married anymore, she took that in stride. It was relatively easy for her to adjust to that abandonment because it felt familiar. The more traumatic experience for her was her husband's aggressive attack on her character as he sought full custody of their children. It is the things that we cannot imagine, cannot imagine ourselves doing, or cannot imagine might happen to us that are the land mines for trauma.

One of the age-old questions among people in challenging situations is, "How could this happen?" and more specifically, "How could God let this happen?" These questions create a relational dilemma that can cause people to go into an endless negative or fearful thought loop. Our minds look for exit points from fear, but the haste to exit the loop can lead to untrue and unhelpful conclusions. Sometimes we have untrue thoughts about ourselves such as "I should have seen it coming." Other times we come to untrue thoughts about God.

Misunderstanding God's character can lead our imaginations to dark and unhelpful places.

Some misunderstandings about God can lead our imaginations into dark and unhelpful places. Claire was a good example of that dynamic. As she was working through her childhood trauma, she started to doubt that God cared about her, and that led to her believing that God must hate her because He let her experience so much abuse. From that point, it was a quick jump to thinking, "Since my therapist aligns with God, she must hate me too."

With our brains so heavily geared to homeostasis, we need some way to move our imaginations and story-telling in new directions. When I was young, I remember my dad saying he was "the black sheep" in his family. As a family therapist, I wonder who started that story. Was "the black sheep" a story he heard from some outside source, and he applied that label to himself because it seemed to match his experience? Maybe someone in his family explicitly said he was "the black sheep." Or, perhaps even more insidious, people told him that he was like one of his uncles, and since that uncle was "the black sheep," my dad effectively inherited that label. The innate human ability for circular logic is both fantastic and terrible. The process of investigating, interrupting, and replacing negative self-fulfilling prophecies is where faith, creativity, and EMDR work beautifully together.

Investigating, interrupting, and replacing negative self-fulfilling prophecies is where faith, creativity, & EMDR work beautifully together.

The big goal of EMDR therapy is to reduce a client's distressed reactions to target memories and things that remind the client of the memory. An EMDR target may or may not be a specific event memory. Distressing body sensations, beliefs, fearful or repetitive thoughts, particular sounds, textures, mouth-feel of foods, smells, and tastes are all viable EMDR targets. The mind also creates "future scenario" memories during prediction generation. I find this interesting because the logical brain often knows that an imagined scene is not "real" in that is has not been experienced physically, but the emotional brain often cannot make that distinction. Throughout the book, I use the words "target," "target memory," and "memory" interchangeably when discussing EMDR therapy.

The remaining chapters are roughly but not precisely aligned with the EMDR therapy process. The eight phases of EMDR therapy are:

1. History taking (learning the client's story and distressing memories)
2. Preparation (establishing sufficient emotional and spiritual resources to give the client strength and courage before confronting upsetting memories)
3. Assessment (deciding on a target memory and doing "setup" for the "BLS" phase)
4. Desensitization (using BLS to reduce negative thoughts, emotions, and body sensations associated with the memory)
5. Installation (adding new adaptive thoughts and emotions to the memory)
6. Body Scan (checking for body sensations that disagree with the installation components)
7. Closure (wrapping up the EMDR session)
8. Reassessment (checking in to see if the changes from the BLS have been maintained and determining whether to continue work on the same target memory or identify and assess a different target)

Part of therapeutic creativity is the blending of multiple therapy models and techniques. The next few pages provide an overview of the other four therapeutic approaches referenced later in the book: Systems Therapy, Christian counseling, Behavioral Therapy, and Art Therapy.

Systems therapy (which includes Family Therapy) refers to working with people in the context of their relationships, the idea being that patterns of thought and behavior somehow serve the individual's drive to either be protected or get their needs met in a particular setting. I also see systems therapy extending to a person's relationship with themselves and God. If we go back to the idea of the mind as a prediction generator, our interactions with self, others, and God turn into stories designed to keep us from pain. Unfortunately, we sometimes draw the wrong conclusions or learn something untrue or only partially true. Sin (from the Hebrew word hamartia) may be defined as "missing the mark" or "to err, be mistaken." We unknowingly set ourselves up for emotional pain when erroneous beliefs underlie our internal stories.

Erroneous beliefs set us up for emotional pain.

Christian counseling refers to how I assess the client's stage of spiritual development, focusing on the relationship with Jesus and the application of Biblical teaching to the client's life. This component is essential because, unlike post-modernism, which says there is no objective truth, the Bible teaches us that there is truth, and we need this grounding point to identify errors in our thinking. I believe prayer adds a lot of power to the healing process, but I want to find out whether the client is open to having spoken prayer in the sessions.

From behavioral counseling, I draw on the Transtheoretical Model (TTM) of behavioral change, more commonly known as The Stages of Change Model. The stages are:

1. Precontemplation: Observers may see a problem, but the client does not see or acknowledge that the problem exists.
2. Contemplation: The client recognizes a problem but has little interest in changing.
3. Preparation: The client is talking about what change might look like, but may not have a clear plan or sufficient motivation yet.
4. Action: The client is implementing a plan to resolve the problem.
5. Maintenance: The client has made a change and the problem is no longer evident.

I like The Stages of Change approach because it normalizes reluctance to change and helps identify where someone is in their readiness to "leap" into the unknown. My client, Claire, sat with me for almost two years, wavering between the Contemplation and Preparation phases. Her decision to finally end our relationship indicated at least a temporary shift into the Action phase.

Knowing where a client stands in readiness to change is key to the therapist's choice of approach. A client who just recognized the problem may be overwhelmed if the therapist moves too quickly into action planning. Similarly, a client fully prepared for change will likely be frustrated by a therapist who engages in reflective listening but does not help develop a feasible plan.

NOTE: Because EMDR and TTM both use the word "Preparation," I will refer to Phase 2 of EMDR as "Resourcing" in later chapters.

The last component is <u>therapeutic art</u>. Although there are many different art-based techniques, most art-making in my office is either drawing or watercolor painting. In addition to free-form art and scribble drawing exercises, I recently added the NeuroGraphica drawing method to my repertoire. Although taught as a future-focused coaching method, NeuroGraphica is surprisingly effective at creating new neural connections and promoting positive emotional and behavioral changes.

While metaphors and positive imagination exercises do not technically fall under therapeutic art, I mention them here because they are powerful creative tools. Creative techniques often help clients access parts of memory and emotion that words can't reach, inviting the client into deeper levels of change and growth.

Combining systems theory, Christian counseling, stages of change, and creativity techniques within the EMDR process allows flexibility in addressing complex client cases. However, it is easy to get lost in the client's chaos without at least a general theory about the underlying problem and how the current symptoms are adaptive.

CHAPTER FIVE

MAKING SENSE OF THE CHAOS

Case conceptualization starts with history taking, but refining continues throughout the therapy process. Although I generally rely on systemic theory, I particularly appreciate Bowenian family therapy because it addresses the fact that patterns subconsciously reproduce themselves from generation to generation. It helps explain how each person's role helps maintain family/system homeostasis even when detrimental to the individual. This model marries quite well with the Christian Bible, which is rich in teaching on family dynamics: how people gain entry into God's family, God's relationship with his adopted children, relationships between family members, the ways that generational patterns emerge, and how to break from the patterns that cause and perpetuate suffering.

Patterns are the foundation of the mind. Patterns allow us to recognize familiar versus unfamiliar, good versus bad, and safe versus unsafe. Understanding our thought and belief patterns helps us make sense of our instinctual reactions so we can slow down and choose informed responses. For this reason, during my initial meeting with a new client, I routinely ask why they are seeking counseling, and then I start building a genogram, the therapeutic version of a family tree. The genogram helps reveal the roles, patterns, and disruptions that built the client's belief system. I am not trying to blame everything on "mom," but I do believe that every behavior starts as an adaptation to meet needs. Exploring past and present networks of relationships, conflicts, religious experiences, and behavioral rules helps me understand the client's default role and understanding of the world.

Clients' exposures to religion and personal faith journeys influence their automatic thoughts and behavioral patterns. To assess the impact of religion and spirituality on a client's story, I want to know what they believe and where they are in their spiritual development. Since I never know how a client will respond to questions about religion and spirituality, I introduce the topic on my client intake form. I ask these two questions: "What are your spiritual beliefs?" and "Do you have any struggles or negative experiences related to faith, spirituality, or religion?" These questions have been great conversation starters, but spiritual assessment can be a landmine.

About two months after starting my practice in Washington, DC, I had a pleasant introductory call with a potential client. He decided to start the therapy process with me, so I sent him the intake paperwork. I received an angry phone call from him just a few hours later. He was furious with me, stating that I should have told him that I was doing religious counseling and that he would not work with me. I was shocked and confused because those two questions on the intake form were the only references to spirituality or religion. I try to make it abundantly clear that each client can choose whether to discuss faith issues. This man was enraged just by the written questions.

I know that I should expect some adverse reactions. Jesus was very blunt about that. He said, "If the world hates you, know that it has hated me before it hated you." John 15:18. I tend to forget about spiritual warfare, so I often feel shocked when it hits me in the face like that. However, from a case conceptualization perspective, that man's overreaction to the questions is a flag in the sand. There's a landmine there. Investigating a client's overreaction tendencies is one way to identify potential EMDR targets.

After that experience, I adjusted my free pre-counseling consultation process and now ask if the prospective client is seeking Christian counseling. If they say 'no,' I reassure them that we do not need to include that in their counseling process. Some people still opt out of working with me because of my faith, but no one else has called to yell at me about those intake questions.

If a client is not closed off to the topic of faith and religion, I gently explore their attitude about God, the gospel message, and people with different spiritual beliefs. I want to know first whether the client believes God exists (yes, no, or unsure), and if the answer is 'yes,' I seek answers to the following questions.

1. What do they believe about Jesus?
2. What is their attitude about attending church and/ or Bible studies? Is it obligatory, a social event, or is there a desire to worship God?
3. Did they make a public profession of faith and choose baptism (versus parental decision)?
4. Was there a time when their relationship with Jesus felt personal? Is that true presently?
5. Does the person pray daily? If so, is it mostly talking at God, or is there a listening component? How does the person receive information and guidance from God?
6. Does the person read or study the Bible or do they get all their information from sermons and other commentaries?
7. What do they believe about the Holy Spirit?
8. Do they believe that God is good all the time?
9. What do they believe about why God allows struggle and suffering?

If a client reports that they believe that God is good or that Jesus is on their side, I highlight that resource, particularly if they don't trust me or feel ambivalent about counseling. Sometimes, I ask the client if they want to pause and pray to ask God to take control of the counseling process. Prayer serves two purposes at this point in the process: it brings the client's attention to God's presence and participation in the process, and it protects because I certainly don't have perfect wisdom. I need the Holy Spirit to guide me.

Prayer brings the client's attention to God's presence and participation in the process.

Dr. Benjamin Keyes authored *The HEART Model: An Integrated Faith-based and Psychological Approach to Heal from Trauma and Produce Balance in the Mind, Body, and Spirit.* His book provides a specific research-backed therapy model for complex trauma, which focuses on helping people connect relationally with God regardless of their thoughts or experiences with church or particular denominations. His model works well with EMDR and may be helpful if you are looking for structured guidance on how to help people connect authentically with God.

As much as we might want someone to connect authentically with God, developing trust between client and therapist is essential. Rapport and trust are the sentiments behind 1 Corinthians 13:1, which says, "If I speak in the tongues of men and of angels, but have not love, I am a noisy gong or a clanging cymbal." If the client does not believe that you care about them as a person and desire to help alleviate their specific pain, your words of wisdom will be an annoying noise.

One of my goals in exploring the client's current, historical, and spiritual context is to reach a point where I can genuinely say, "Wow! Given that environment, it makes sense that you started this behavior. I can see how that helped preserve your sense of self." Sometimes, that statement is the first time anyone has validated the client's experience, and it is not uncommon to see tears of relief in a client's eyes.

Although my counseling coursework included instruction on history-taking, I learned the most about history-taking from an experience during my internship in Houston. In Texas, specific state-funded agencies offer free addiction treatment assessments to funnel clients into treatment programs. The primary goals are to determine the type of care (outpatient, intensive outpatient, partial hospitalization, or in-patient) that is the best fit for the client's substance abuse patterns and daily obligations and find a suitable treatment program for the client to start as soon as possible. The process requires approximately three hours.

I only observed one assessment session, but I was awed by the counselor's ability to elicit information from the client. It was not a dry, formulaic interview. In many moments, it sounded like a pleasant chat between new friends. Periodically, the client said something that caught the counselor's attention, initiating a more in-depth exploration for a few minutes before returning to the client's central narrative. As a new therapist, two specific aspects of the interaction caught my attention. First, I could tell that the counselor was genuinely interested in the client as a person. I saw the client relax when the counselor acknowledged her courage to seek help and tell her story. Second, the counselor allowed the client to tell her story naturally. He could have forced the conversation to follow the order of the assessment questions as shown in the computer system. Instead, he prioritized rapport and adjusted his note-taking to match the client's story-telling style. Similarly, successful management of EMDR cases requires balancing between the client's story-telling pace and keeping the sessions on track to complete memory processing.

Pace with the client
Manage the focus
Trust the process

Listening closely to discover underlying messages and motivations is an important part of EMDR therapy. A skilled EMDR therapist listens for "good fuel" and "bad fuel" for the prediction generator. Good fuel allows the mind to take in all information, allowing for more accurate interpretations of events and flexibility in problem-solving while "bad fuel" maintains negative prediction cycles. Exceptions to the client's negative beliefs are potential bridges to healing. Similarly, exploring alternative interpretations can build new off-ramps from the client's negative thought patterns.

I had an interesting alternate interpretation moment with a client, "Eddie," who was baffled by his recent unethical behavior. Eddie spoke of how he justified his behavior after the fact but felt confused about his underlying motivation. As we discussed his job situation, Eddie stated, "I am the one who is always available." Just before Eddie's behavior changed, several co-workers unexpectedly took time off or significantly reduced their work hours. When the reduced manpower extended beyond a couple of weeks, the managers could have changed deadlines or adjusted expectations. Instead, Eddie's workload tripled, and he received criticism for missing deadlines. I suddenly had an insight into his behavior change and am thankful that the Holy Spirit provided a new perspective. I told him, "Eddie, your brain was trying to help you. It said, 'Since no one is listening to your objections, I know exactly how to get you out of this situation. This bad behavior will make them see you differently, and no one will expect so much from you!'" Even if not wholly accurate, this alternate perspective prompted a discussion about secondary gains, a discussion Eddie had rejected earlier in the session. He later revealed that the session went better than expected because I had been curious and interested in looking for the underlying motive rather than shaming him for bad behavior.

It is easy to forget that shame is a powerful deterrent to seeking help. Therapists' reactions to client stories can reinforce or alleviate shame. In my own experience as a client, I almost let shame prevent me from talking to my therapist about a troubling thought. At odd moments, the thought, "I don't want to be here," kept popping into my mind even though I did not feel suicidal. I was afraid that my counselor would assume that I was suicidal and that her worry for me would prevent her from listening to me. To her credit, she stayed curious and listened as I enumerated all the places, roles, and circumstances I wished to escape. After listening for a while, she said, "You don't sound depressed. You sound angry." That shocked me into stillness for a moment. It was a profoundly helpful adjustment for my prediction generator.

Depression is a stuck, trapped place fueled by the belief that "nothing will ever change," but anger opens up a whole new realm of possibilities. It made me reconsider how I interpreted my circumstances and my body's reactions. Even though we were still in the history-taking phase, the transformation process began because she sparked my curiosity and creativity. Her reflections on my story provided me with a new perspective to explore in pursuit of my therapy goals.

As a therapist, I feel excited when I have clarity about a client's situation and a general set of goals. It feels like a treasure hunt.

My husband and I have gone on many treasure-hunting adventures, from combing Maryland beaches for shark teeth to sifting through Arkansas mud for diamonds. Mushroom-hunting excursions are by far our most frequent and adventurous outings. We usually choose a specific place to explore, but one day, he said, "Let's drive north and see if we can find mushrooms." I asked where we were going. He said, "I don't know, but people are finding mushrooms north of us, so let's just go explore." We wandered north from Houston, TX, all the way up to Omaha, NE. It was not a particularly successful mushroom hunt, but we had fun and discovered some interesting places along the way.

Sometimes we know the destination, other times we explore with purpose.

Therapy is similar to mushroom hunting; sometimes, we know the destination, and other times, we explore with the purpose of developing more specific goals. Clarity about the type of journey often occurs during the first history-taking meeting. However, case complexity may delay clarity. I like using a structured case conceptualization process based on Ricky Greenwald's Fairy Tale Model if I feel confused after several sessions. This model has its basis in the hero's journey. The client is the hero

fighting the dragon. The hero's primary goals are to slay the dragon, prevent further dragon attacks, and develop adequate defenses in case another dragon does appear. The role of therapy is to help the client heal from the injuries sustained in the dragon attack, establish effective measures to protect against further attacks, and have appropriate measures to reduce future harm.

Let's pause to explore how to apply the fairy tale approach to a fictional client situation. For this discussion, the client is "Brittney," a woman seeking EMDR therapy because she has chronic throat issues and has a pattern of avoiding care until she must go to the hospital emergency room.

When we explore further, Brittney has been with the same primary care doctor for five years but does not trust him. She has considered finding a different doctor. However, each time Brittney plans to see a new doctor, she gets so anxious that she cancels the appointment. She reports no difficulty attending dental, physical therapy, or counseling appointments. She also denies feeling any loyalty to her primary care doctor. Brittney was in her early 20s the first time she had issues with her vocal cords. Since then, she has had laryngitis at least twice a year. She said that previous counselors helped her manage other anxieties, but Brittney still feels stuck in this one area.

At this point in the process, we can start the case conceptualization but may find some holes in our history-taking. I purposefully left a few question marks in the following example to illustrate this point.

Once upon a time, there was a beautiful young woman. She lived with her parents and two sisters. She felt loved, and many people in her community considered her "the talented daughter."

Life was busy with professional vocal training and theater performances.

But one day, illness struck and she literally lost her voice. And ?

She felt ___ ?

And believed __ ? I am weak?

These thoughts and feelings get stirred up every time her throat hurts.

To protect herself, she avoids doctors as much as possible when she has pain or discomfort in her throat.

This caused new problems because whenever she gets sick, she waits so long to get medical care that she ends up in the hospital.

Brittney told me when and how the throat problems started, but I missed some vital information. Many clients have an internal defense system that will cause a distraction to avoid the discomfort of sharing details about a distressing experience. It is also easy to miss critical information when clients recall their experiences out of chronological order.

The fairy tale format for case conceptualization helps highlight the missing pieces. In this case example, a subsequent conversation revealed that Brittney's first illness resulted in her missing a chance to perform in front of a talent scout. Since the illness ruined her vocal range, she is mourning the death of her singing career dreams. She believes the majority of vocal cord damage was the fault of multiple doctors who diagnosed her sore throat symptoms as "overuse" and missed the underlying infection. Brittney's distrust of medical doctors resulted in more severe illness episodes, which, in turn, made doctors more impatient with her. Adding these additional details to the fairy tale narrative exposes a logical basis for her specific phobia of medical doctors.

The revised case conceptualization also reveals several potential EMDR target, including the client's first illness, the surgery, and the loss of her "big shot." When I present these potential targets to the client, she might identify additional targets, such as "the fight with my mom about having surgery," "the nurse who was mean to me," "feeling betrayed by the friend who auditioned in my spot," etc.

While fine-tuning the previous example, I realized that in some client cases, "the dragon" (the instigating event) is unknown even after additional history taking. In my experience, there are three conditions that tend to hide the instigating event.

1.   Genetics
2.   Early childhood trauma
3.   Pervasive neglect

A genetic trait called Sensory Processing Sensitivity (SPS) can cause high sensitivity to different types of stimuli. Individuals in this subgroup often call themselves Highly Sensitive Persons or HSPs. The presentation of SPS varies widely, and recent research discovered that thousands of genetic variants contribute to this sensitivity (Keers). Given the genome-wide influence, it makes sense that some people struggle with emotion while others struggle more with auditory, visual, or tactile input.

One of the traits of an HSP is that they become overwhelmed easily. Psychologist Tom Falkenstein describes it this way, "Everything that highly sensitive people experience they process deeply, and every experience leaves behind traces in the form of thoughts, feelings, impressions, bodily sensations, memories, and fantasies. It is as if the mind and the body of a highly sensitive person are a seismograph that is able to pick up subtle vibrations in the ground, responding far more quickly and reacting far more strongly."

If your client has HSP traits, perhaps the fairytale dragon is "She was born with SPS." You may ask, "How do I write the 'Once upon a time' section of the fairy tale if the problem started at birth?" That's where an extra dose of creativity is required. Since most people agree that humans have souls and/or spirits that transcend the physical body, the "once upon a time" section of the fairytale can be the story of the client's "real" or "whole" self apart from the hypersensitivity. Naming "SPS" as the dragon helps externalize the problem, puts other events into a more cohesive story, and helps the client figure out how to appreciate their differentness rather than staying in a mode of fear about what might overwhelm them next.

Unfortunately, SPS symptoms are often indistinguishable from a trauma response. Processing a traumatic event is simpler than targeting an inherent trait because an event is clearly outside of the client's personhood. So, if a client has a gut feeling that something bad happened, I assume that there is a trauma memory to target. When trauma occurs at a very young age, a client may have body sensations or intense emotional reactions but no words to describe the event. An unnamed trauma can be the EMDR target, even if there is no physical evidence or corroborating witness.

The client's current-day beliefs, emotional reactivity, and distressing physical sensations are the only details that require specificity for successful EMDR processing. If the client feels distracted or distressed by the lack of visual memory, I have the client imagine seeing a child experiencing the client's symptoms and consider what that child needs to feel safe, secure, and calm.

A few years ago, "Tom" came to me because he had an exaggerated startle response, and certain sounds caused nausea. Based on the sounds that bothered him, Tom suspected that something traumatic happened to him in a doctor's office or hospital. Although the details of the event were unknown, Tom felt his symptoms made him "defective." We used an imagined medical setting as the EMDR target image for desensitization. He later reported that he still disliked the trigger sounds but no longer reacted with nausea.

Unspecific, nagging feelings can also result from childhood neglect. Neglect can result in pervasive loneliness, an inability to trust others, an inability to connect or form attachments, or a pattern of volatile attachments in close interpersonal relationships. Some neglect survivors struggle primarily with family and romantic relationships, while other people are unable to maintain any close relationships (friendships, business partnerships, etc.). Neglect can go on for years or occur for a short but critical period.

There is a whole generation whose parents followed the Ferber method of letting babies cry themselves to sleep. I do not believe that those parents were generally neglectful, but the experts at the time provided harmful advice. Regardless of the motive, letting a baby cry alone for hours ignores the baby's need for physical touch and creates distress and despair when the only means of requesting help (crying) is fruitless. Sometimes, a client's ongoing distress comes from that inconsolable infant part of the client with no words to explain the fear, loneliness, and anxiety. When setting up the case conceptualization for neglect or abandonment experiences, the fairy tale dragon is "being left alone and helpless."

Even normal family transitions can cause neglect or abandonment experiences. It can feel traumatic for a child when an attentive older sibling leaves for college or when a close grandparent or nanny "disappears" due to illness or death. Some children experience neglect when a new baby enters the household, particularly if the mother experiences post-partum depression. These common family transitions often significantly reduce the quality and quantity of attention the child receives from the parents or caregivers. If the child is in a key developmental phase during the time of neglect or perceived abandonment, it can have lasting effects even if attentive parenting resumes. For case conceptualization purposes, you might explore with the client what they feel was more impactful: the general unavailability of the caregiver or a moment of shame/embarrassment resulting from the neglect.

Once you have the full fairytale narrative or complete case conceptualization, potential EMDR targets usually emerge. However, clients who are very guarded may simply not give you enough information or may whitewash the information so that it seems as if nothing significant has happened. Don't be fooled; the client is in your office for a reason. You may need to work on establishing emotional safety and trust and then come back to history taking.

Unclear history or inconsistent timelines within the client's story may also indicate ADHD. Challenges with time management are a common symptom of ADHD, but the difficulty marking time can also cause struggles in remembering and relating events chronologically. This challenge causes some clients a great deal of distress, and in the absence of another clear target, that distress might be a good starting target.

Don't be fooled, the client is in your office for a reason.

For EMDR therapists: if you feel stuck in history taking with a client because there is no clear target or the case conceptualization is still confusing, consider working on history taking and preparation phases simultaneously. I recommend exploring the client's inner world to identify ambivalence about counseling and leading the client through calming and grounding techniques. These techniques reduce anxiety, reveal the client's thought patterns and beliefs, and help fill gaps in the case conceptualization.

With that in mind, let's move on to the Preparation phase, where we discover how dedicated the client is to change.

CHAPTER SIX

PREPARATION
IS THE WORK

Even in highly motivated clients, the stated desire to change and actual willingness to change are often at odds. Sometimes, the preparation is the work. I first heard that statement during a webinar led by Dr. Parnell. Her point was that some clients just won't be ready, willing, or able to process trauma memories, but the preparation for EMDR can vastly improve their lives nonetheless. I have encountered this truth with several of my clients.

I spent months working with one client on her battle with her inner critic, helping her develop compassion for herself. When I felt she was ready for the next EMDR phase, I asked her how she was feeling about the event that brought her to counseling. She responded, "Oh, that's not bothering me anymore." I was skeptical. I suspected that the memory network was isolated from her normal emotional state, preventing her from accessing her feelings about the memory. As it turned out, she was honest with me. There were a few body sensations to desensitize, but all the negative emotions and beliefs had dissolved while we were preparing for memory processing. This client's experience is the exception, not the rule, but I mention it because sometimes a client's internal battle is more problematic than any specific memory. An example of an internal struggle is when a client's health-conscious part says, "I am going to lose my job if I don't get sober, so I must stop drinking," while an anxious part says, "If I stop drinking bad memories will overwhelm me, so I can't stop drinking."

Whether the core issue is an internal conflict or a specific event, the central questions in the preparation phase are "What is the client willing to do or stop doing to heal?" and "What is preventing the wound from healing?" For the remainder of the chapter, I will refer to the second phase of EMDR as "Resourcing" to distinguish it from the Stages of Change model's Preparation stage described below.

The transtheoretical model of behavioral change (TTM), commonly called the Stages of Change Model, offers a means of assessing a client's readiness to change. The stages of change are Precontemplation, Contemplation, Preparation, Action, and Maintenance. Most people are at differing readiness levels across different topics or aspects of life. For example, I can tell you that I am preparing (and sometimes taking action) to meet my physical activity goal each week. However, I am only contemplating eliminating coffee from my diet. If a nutritionist used the stages of change, she might help me develop more consistent physical activity to help me stay in the action stage and move toward the maintenance stage. She believes my caffeine consumption is likely causing problems, but she knows I do not share that belief. Rather than try to talk me into a caffeine reduction plan, she might ask me to log my caffeine intake and my moods and fatigue levels. I might contemplate reducing my caffeine consumption if she can help me see a correlation.

Similarly, a therapist can help clients set realistic goals using the Stages of Change model. Rather than being a pass-or-fail situation, stage-based goal-setting allows space for the client to explore barriers, mentally rehearse new patterns, and celebrate small changes. Minor changes and successes can build the client's confidence and motivation to pursue more extensive changes. Using this model also helps the therapist have more patience with the process because the small shifts are more apparent when the focus is on moving up one stage rather than racing toward the end goal. To add clarity, let's explore each stage in more detail.

Focus on moving up one stage rather than racing to the end goal.

Precontemplation

A person in the Precontemplation stage is either unable or unwilling to see that there's a problem that they need to solve. If they acknowledge a problem exists, they claim it is someone else's problem. In counseling vernacular, a Precontemplation client is not the actual customer. There is someone else in their life who has pushed or mandated the counseling. The therapist's work in this phase is to join with the client, validate their experience, and let the client settle in enough to start considering any internal disagreement with their story.

For example, a client might say: "I have to use drugs to stay calm because my girlfriend is always picking fights and creating drama. Even if I do exactly what she wants, she tells me I did it wrong."

The therapist responds: "Wow, that sounds like a really stressful environment. I can see why you feel the need to escape sometimes."

Client: "Yeah, I don't know why I'm with her; she makes my life so hard."

Th: "It sounds as if you're wondering whether it's worth staying in that relationship."

Ct: "Yeah, I mean, I feel like I kind of owe it to her because she put up with so much of my BS."

Th: "Huh. So, you feel like you deserve some of her criticism because of things you did before?"

Ct: "I guess, yeah. But she's relentless; there's never a peaceful moment. I just have to chill out sometimes."

Notice that the client briefly acknowledged that he may be part of the problem but quickly moved back to blaming the girlfriend. That's the work in the precontemplation phase — giving the client space to feel the conflict and the weight of responsibility for their actions until they decide it might be worth considering a change.

Contemplation

A client in Contemplation accepts some responsibility for the problem but feels ambivalent about whether it's worth the effort to try to change anything. It's essential to look for secondary gain for this client's issues. Secondary gains are hidden advantages for an otherwise unwanted behavior. Returning to the internal battle example at the start of this chapter, the client wanted to stop drinking to save her job. The client's belief that alcohol protects her from being emotionally overwhelmed is the secondary gain of her alcoholism. As an EMDR therapist, I might ask the client, "If we could make the bad memories less intense, would that change your feelings about getting sober?" This question encourages the client to imagine a new way of living without alcohol or emotional overwhelm. Similarly, a socially isolated client might want to develop closer relationships, but her past experiences of feeling abandoned prevent her from trusting other people. Protection from abandonment is the secondary gain in this case. Helping the client recover from past abandonments frees the client to move into the preparation phase for developing closer friendships.

Preparation

The Preparation stage begins when the client recognizes a need to change but lacks sufficient plan, motivation, or confidence to make the change. There is often ambivalence in this stage when a plan feels too daunting. Much of the EMDR Resourcing work happens when the client is in the Preparation stage of change. Here, we explore all the things (internal and external) that might help or hinder the change process. More importantly, it is here that the client must decide whether they are willing to sacrifice their current known pain for an unknown future.

Action

Action is the implementation of the plan. The lines between stages of change and EMDR are not as evident here. I think that memory processing is usually part of the Action stage, but there are some clients for whom memory processing is still part of the preparation for a more significant life change. The therapist's role at this point is to encourage the client's efforts, celebrate successes, and facilitate navigation of potential setbacks.

Maintenance

The Maintenance phase represents the continuation of the new, changed state as modified thought and behavior patterns become "the new normal." Some people can continue in this phase indefinitely. The goal of EMDR is to get people into a Maintenance phase of healing and forgiveness, and in many cases, this is a reasonable goal.

Relapse

The Relapse phase was added to the Stages of Change model to more accurately represent and normalize the substance abuse addiction cycle. Relapse occurs when the client returns to the old behavior or pattern, which takes the client back to the Contemplation phase. Some clients stay in Contemplation for an extended time, but others can rebound through the stages and settle again into Maintenance.

I had one EMDR case that I can honestly label a failure. The client, "Ron," had obsessive thoughts that led him to compulsively wash his hands and avoid germs. The symptoms were so severe that sometimes it took him multiple hours to complete a simple cleaning task. I provided EMDR therapy to him for about a year, but each time we reached a breakthrough, Ron's severe compulsive symptoms reemerged. Eventually, I realized I needed to talk to Ron about the future. We had discussed his life dreams but not his path to that goal. In the follow-up conversation, I learned that Ron depended on disability benefits to pay rent. If his symptoms became well managed, he would lose the disability benefits. If his benefits ended before he was financially stable, he could end up homeless. He was unwilling to take that risk. So, although he moved briefly into other stages of change, Ron ultimately settled back into the Contemplation stage.

In the previous chapter, I mentioned my experience observing an addiction treatment assessment. That assessment interview was my first experience witnessing the stages of change in action. Part of the interview included an inventory of substances the client used and abused and a rating of her readiness to change. That particular client was seeking help with her alcohol abuse and felt some ambivalence about her treatment options because she wanted to keep her job. When exploring the client's use of other substances, she reported that she used marijuana weekly but saw no problem with the frequency or quantity of her use. In contrast, she was highly motivated to stop using nicotine because she felt smoking cigarettes contributed to her alcohol cravings.

At that point in my career, I believed it was important for the client to quit all substances, so my impulse was to label her attitude about marijuana as 'resistance.' Fortunately, the counselor conducting that interview explained the stages of change and why the client might fear changing everything at once. The client's mind predicted that if she quit all substances at the same time, her world would collapse, so it was safer to maintain some of her coping measures for the time being. The mind knows that the safest way off a ten-story scaffolding is climbing down one story at a time, not jumping from the top.

Unfortunately, even when clients are ready for change, they may not trust the therapy process or the therapist. When introducing a client to EMDR, it is not unusual to encounter some hesitation from the client. This hesitation is partly a prediction generator failure. Because EMDR is unfamiliar, it is difficult for the client to imagine how it might be helpful. However, hesitation may also indicate the client's distrust of the therapist. If we are too quick to dismiss a client's distrust or hesitation, this can come back in unhelpful and damaging ways later in the process.

Since clients are often not tuned into why they feel distrustful or unsafe, I usually engage the client in internal exploration exercises. I like to use BLS during this process. It provides a gentle introduction to BLS while identifying fear and addressing pessimistic predictions about EMDR. My theory is that using BLS with the client's internal parts also provides some desensitization of anxiety about the EMDR process.

Clients are often not tuned into why they feel emotionally unsafe.

The general idea behind internal parts work is that there are parts of our personality that try to protect us when we feel attacked, parts that we deem undesirable based on cultural norms, and parts that try to avoid pain. Sometimes, the desire to avoid pain results in ignoring the internal parts that hold shame, embarrassment, or any other uncomfortable emotions. Each client identifies their internal parts uniquely. Some parts are designated by role (child, sibling, parent, professional). Other clients divide parts according to ages that feel pivotal (age 5, age 12, college age, etc.) or by emotional state or role in the client's well-being (happy, sad, angry, needy, responsible, carefree). One of my particularly fragmented clients had a separate part for every traumatic event in her life.

Some clients react negatively to the idea of "parts" or "inner child," so I try to find language that the client accepts. Often, the easiest entry point is discussing the client's different roles in life. Most people agree that they act slightly differently at work versus out on the softball field, hanging out with siblings, or dealing with their parents. I usually ask the client if they will try a brief visualization experiment with me. "Experiment" is another word I find helpful to scoot around client anxiety. An experiment is allowed to fail; it's just an accepted part of that paradigm, and it gives the therapist a chance to figure out what resonates with the client and seek collaboration from that perspective.

The internal exploration tool I use most often is "the internal conference room" activity. In my Washington, DC practice, I have primarily high-achieving professional clients. They spend a lot of time in meetings and conference rooms where they have learned to be emotionally guarded and hypervigilant because of adversarial and predatory colleagues. Since I want them to drop their guard and be honest with themselves and me, I have dropped the "conference room" label and instead refer to this exercise as "the internal gathering place."

I introduce this activity by saying that we all have different versions of ourselves that show up in various settings—divided by role (sister, friend, boss), skill (musician, problem solver, rescuer), age, or internal function (holding fun memories, holding pain, scanning for danger, managing expectations, criticizing dumb ideas, etc.). Some people think I am too directive in this activity, but I prefer to err by giving too many suggestions rather than letting the client "fail" or get frustrated at this point. Although strengthening rapport is a primary goal, the exercise helps clients tune into their deeper emotions and beliefs.

Experiments give us permission to fail.

The setup for the internal gathering place is similar to a creative writing prompt such as "Tell a story about a conflict at summer camp." The setup boosts the client's imagination about what "parts" exist within themselves. Then, I lead them through the following steps so they can create additional imaginal details.

We all have different versions of ourselves...

First, I ask the client to imagine a place where all their parts, or versions of self, can meet. The imagined space can be formal, like a board room, informal, like a living room or game room, or even outdoors. I ask the client what comes to their mind so I can refer to that place later.

Next, I instruct the client to imagine being there and invite the other versions of self into that space. I pause for a moment while they get into that image.

Then, I ask the client to notice if any parts or versions are missing. If parts are missing, I ask the client to investigate why that part does not want to participate and see if they can provide encouragement or reassurance. Some clients talk to me as they visualize, but if they don't, I usually ask if they feel stuck or if all the parts are in the space.

Once the client says the gathering feels complete, I ask if any internal parts are worried, upset, or angry about the idea of counseling in general and EMDR specifically. This process allows me to address any latent anger, fear, or disbelief that might derail the healing.

At this point in the discussion, the client's point of view may change. The client might speak actively from the perspective of feeling fear, anger, or disbelief. Or the client might answer from a detached state on behalf of a distressed part. The difference in language is "I'm worried" (embodiment) versus "that part feels" (detached state). There is nothing inherently wrong about either type of answer. I use the response as a diagnostic tool, assessing whether the client defaults into the observational realm versus dropping into their emotion. This information helps me know whether the client might need help letting themselves feel or if they need help stepping back into an observational perspective during later memory processing.

When a client indicates discomfort, fear, or anger about being in counseling or trying EMDR, I keep the conversation light and curious to avoid further agitation. I ask what would make that internal part comfortable with counseling or EMDR. During this exercise, four general categories of responses emerge.

What if it doesn't work?

Clients frequently ask about the process or logistics of memory processing. I answer these questions as simply and directly as possible since I do not know the emotional maturity of the protective part. Protective parts are often afraid to hope that EMDR will help; they have been disappointed before. In this type of situation, I invite the client to try an experiment with me — just to see what might happen — not expecting a miracle, just being curious about what might come to mind during memory processing.

This might be too scary.

Vulnerable or victim parts may feel unsafe because the memory still feels threatening. I address this directly by discussing the goal of watching the memory from a distance and not re-living it. If that instruction and reassurance fail to alleviate the fear, then we pause here to work on developing internal protectors. As a Christian, I believe spiritual guidance and protection come from outside of myself via the Holy Spirit. In contrast, the Internal Family Systems theory posits that we have different parts of ourselves that protect us from possible pain and distract us from perceived pain.

I utilize both perspectives using four approaches to enhance perceived safety:

1. Invite a spiritual protector to provide help or comfort to the fearful part,
2. Employ stronger parts as protectors of vulnerable parts,
3. Create/install a new protector or nurturing figure,
4. Permit the fearful parts to stay shielded in a fun and/or safe place during memory processing.

At times, I use all four of these approaches with the same client, particularly if the client has complex PTSD or does not have memories of stable, available, and emotionally safe caregivers or protective figures.

What if the change is bad or unsafe?

It is natural for the client to fear "getting well." After all, our internal defense systems usually focus on reducing uncertainty. If the client no longer fears the memory, the client's internal world must find a new focus. Angry, protective parts often fear that healing will result in their obsolescence and banishment. At the same time, other parts fear that new responsibilities will be overwhelming. Discussing these fears provides an opportunity to explore assigning new roles for the internal parts and create collaboration between the parts. It is also an opportunity for the client to invite God, Jesus, or the Holy Spirit into the process.

When a protector part is in overdrive, the client may believe that remaining upset about a particular trauma event protects them from future trauma events because they will see the bad things coming. I use a martial arts metaphor to address this concern. A trained fighter must be ready to move and recognize real threats versus benign elements or individuals. If they ignore their surroundings, they might get blindsided. However, if they misinterpret everything as a threat, they may turn their back on the real threat and still get blindsided. An appropriate level exists in the middle, ignoring benign elements and being ready to respond to attacks from credible threats. From this perspective, most clients agree that releasing extra vigilance could help.

A container activity can help the client maintain healthy vigilance before desensitizing or releasing excess fear, anxiety, or energy. The client first thinks about the skills, emotions, or attributes necessary to stay safe or do their job well and then imagines placing those things in a sealed container safe from disturbance until needed. This imaginal exercise reinforces the client's active role in deciding what internal protections they still need and what they are ready to release. They are "participating in" rather than being "subjected to" the EMDR process.

Let's just do it.

Some clients and their parts are so ready to start desensitizing memories that they are annoyed with me for spending so much time discussing the process. I usually address impatience by validating their desire to feel better and thanking them for their willingness to bear with me during this investigation phase. I often say, "I just want to ensure that all parts of you are on board with the plan now so they do not undermine your progress later." Most people can see the wisdom in this approach because they have experienced self-sabotaging moments.

My final goal in the EMDR Resourcing phase is to have the client identify and develop an internal resource team and a safe/calm place. I want to ensure the client can willfully access their creativity for something positive instead of endlessly looping through all the terrible things that might happen.

Can the client willfully access their creativity for positive purposes?

The "Nurturer, Protector, and Wisdom figure" exercise sparks the client's creativity by visualizing an internal support team. The basic framework asks the client to think of a figure representing each category. The word "figure" is helpful because some people get caught up in the idea that they have to think of someone from their life. It is often unhelpful when the client chooses a "real person" because every relationship experiences disconnects and disappointments. In contrast, a figure can be anything or any character representing the category; it could be an animal, a historical figure, or a character from a book or movie. Clients often have questions about the definition of "nurturing" or "protecting." I try to let the client answer the question by asking, "What kind of nurturing or protecting would help you cope with looking at painful memories?"

One teenage client could not think of any figures for this activity. When my general examples did not help, I changed tactics. I asked him about what kinds of stories he liked. He told me that he did not read books or watch TV. I asked, "What do you like to do?" He named a video game that he enjoys. As he explained the characters in the game, I commented on which characters seemed like protectors, which were nurturers, etc. Once those labels were attached to something familiar, he came up with other familiar figures and selected his internal support team.

To finalize the internal support team, the client imagines receiving nurturing, protection, and help from the support team. The real power of this process is its ability to bypass the brain's logic center. If I ask someone, "Are you nurturing?" or "Are you protective?" Most will answer in a "yes, but" fashion, which mutes or minimizes their belief in those strengths. By creating internal parts to hold each strength, the client can access those skills without resistance from weak, ineffective, or doubtful parts.

Imagining separate parts helps the client hold opposing ideas and bypass the all-or-nothing thinking in the brain's logic center.

This activity is also an opportunity to assess whether the client's theology is a help or hindrance to healing. If the client does not choose a spiritual figure for any categories, I ask if they want to add one. On more than one occasion, a client said yes and reported feeling much better after adding the spiritual support. Asking the client about adding a spiritual support figure can be a pivotal moment in the client's spiritual growth. The client must make a deliberate decision to include or exclude God as a source of support or comfort in the healing process.

Is the client's theology helping or hurting?

In addition to the three protector figures, I lead the client through a "Safe/Calm Place" visualization. Clients often choose an outdoor setting such as a forest, a mountain top, or a beach. If I have not seen the client change emotional states during history taking, I engage them in a practice exercise. I ask the client to think of something mildly annoying, like the traffic light that skips your lane for a cycle or something they find disgusting. After accessing the unpleasant memory, I ask the client to imagine being in the "Safe/Calm Place" until their body and emotions are neutral or positive. We repeat this process several times until the client quickly shifts between emotional states. This is important because it shows the client that they can shift away from distressing thoughts and memories. It also gives me a way to prompt the client back to a calm state if they become overwhelmed during memory processing.

The EMDR Resourcing phase may require a single session, but some clients need extra time here. Early in my career, I attended a few crisis intervention training classes taught by the late Jack Nowicki. He often said that clients in crisis are "discombobulated" and, therefore, need the therapist to lend their frontal cortex to normalize and help create an action plan. For clients who are anxious, chaotic, and "discombobulated," I spend extra time demystifying the EMDR process and explaining what I'm doing and why. Managing the client's anxiety leads back to preparation throughout the EMDR process, sometimes just as a reminder of the preparation already done, sometimes as a pause to add more resources.

Some clients start every session in the Preparation Stage of Change. My client "Becky" sat across from me at our first meeting and said, "I'm only coming for twelve sessions." That took me aback, but I thought, "Okay, let's see what we can do with twelve sessions; this should be fine." I discovered over the first two sessions that Becky was skeptical about therapy, unsure whether it was a good idea to explore her emotions, and reluctant to trust anyone, including me. Over time, she showed signs of trusting me but remained guarded about her change process.

I had to accept that Becky would not admit to changing her mind or perspective during counseling sessions. Even when she relaxed during a session, Becky's armor was back in place by the next appointment. It took fifteen to twenty minutes for her to relax her defensive posture each time we met. I have to credit God because I have no idea how we went through this dance every session and still had time for memory processing. Eventually, I decided my main job was seed planting with Becky. At first, when I provided a reframe (an alternate interpretation of a situation), her response was either outright rejection of the idea or silence. One day, I was shocked when Becky responded, "Maybe."

By meeting her each session in a contemplation/preparation stage, we finally reached a point where she did not immediately reject my input. Eventually, she ended each session with, "I'll think about it." As stoic as she is, I had a few enjoyable moments when Becky smirked at me because we both knew she had made a breakthrough, but she wouldn't admit it verbally. Incidentally, she also stayed well beyond those first twelve sessions.

When I first met Becky, I thought she resisted change until outside pressure forced her hand. However, she proved me wrong. There was a point when she decided she had had enough of her stagnant life and actively sought a change. She collapsed back into her despondent overthinking pattern when things did not work out as she hoped. Still, she gave me a glimpse of what was possible for her. It helped me to continue cheering for her because she showed that initiative. Her initiative gave me hope because it showed me that any of us can be proactive under the right circumstances. There's just the question of whether we have enough strength and scaffolding to maintain that posture.

Blocking beliefs prevent us from seriously entertaining change.

Resiliency scaffolding is often undermined by blocking beliefs. A blocking belief is a story the client tells herself that prevents her from seriously entertaining or adopting change. When a client does not acknowledge the internal resistance, it creates an interesting therapeutic dynamic. In one case, a client, "Amy," started pressuring me to "do EMDR" (referring to memory processing). Each time I tried to identify a target, she derailed the setup process by lamenting over the same few situations and resisting my efforts to redirect the discussion. Amy told me she wanted to do EMDR, but her behavior in the session told me the opposite.

Eventually, I had the full setup done for a target memory. I decided to see if desensitization might get her more in tune with her body and bypass the victimhood narrative. We did not complete the memory processing, but we did identify Amy's blocking belief, "I missed God's plan for my life."

At that point, I redirected the session, asking Amy to close her eyes and imagine sitting in God's presence. As she did that, I spoke words affirming God's love for her, her identity as God's daughter, and how she radiates God's love through her kindness toward the people under her care. A few weeks later, I noticed a shift in Amy's language. She used positive language as she talked about the future. She was still uncertain about the next step in her career, but she seemed excited about the possibilities.

In summary, much good work can occur in the Resourcing phase of EMDR. If you have a good rapport with the client, are familiar with their defense mechanisms, and know that the client has some capacity to self-soothe, it's worth at least attempting specific memory processing. The process is pretty forgiving, so if the client needs more preparation or resourcing, you can return to this phase anytime.

CHAPTER SEVEN

SETTING
THE
STAGE

The next EMDR phase is the assessment (of a particular memory), but before we go there in Chapter 8, let's pause to discuss the final treatment planning stage. Unless the client is in therapy for a particular event, like a car accident or a burglary, EMDR target memories need to be named, categorized, and prioritized. In previous chapters, I suggested various ways of identifying potential EMDR targets during the case conceptualization and preliminary treatment planning. The most important part of treatment planning is getting the client to agree on the specific memories or themes to address.

The EMDR Basic Training I attended taught therapists to ask the client to name three to five bothersome or distressing memories. This instruction came with the caveat of not letting the client get into the memory but moving quickly from one memory to the next, only pausing long enough to get a "title" for the memory and a zero to ten rating of the subjective unit of disturbance (SUD), where ten is the highest level of distress. The SUD asks how intensely the client feels about the memory right now (or how intense it would feel if they let themselves think about it) instead of how intense the event felt when it occurred. The instructor stressed, over and over again, the importance of not letting the client get into each memory. I struggle with this approach because it teaches the therapist to fear the client's emotions. Overall, I don't think there's anything wrong with asking the client to identify potential targets. However, this rushed list-making approach causes me anxiety and interrupts my rapport with clients. So, to keep everyone engaged and moving forward, I ditched the formulaic list-making.

Over time, I discovered that my clients seem to experience faster progress when we identify targets through the client's present-day concerns instead of the quick-list process. There are two reasons why it helps to start with current issues. First, the client experiences more immediate relief rather than ignoring current pain to process old memories. Second, when starting from a current distress point, the mind often takes the client to memories they did not recognize as problematic and, therefore, would not be on the target list. This emergence of unexpected connections happened to me when I was a therapy client.

About a year ago, I engaged in an EMDR session because I felt excluded from friend gatherings here in DC. This feeling took me back to when I was boxed out by friends when I was about fifteen years old. This connection is not surprising because it was a very similar feeling. But then my mind took an unexpected turn. The next thing that came up was resentment about my family's move from Winslow, Arizona, to Scottsdale, Arizona, when I was eleven. My therapist helped me see that I had a similar unresolved frustration about moving from Texas to DC ten years ago. If someone asked me to list my problematic childhood memories, "leaving Winslow" would not have made the list, yet that memory anchored my exclusion struggles.

I realize that I am defaulting my counseling methods to what has worked best for me as a client, and there is a certain level of bias there. At the same time, since human brains are all wired for the same essential functions and all have subconscious networks connecting ideas, letting the subconscious mind lead the way to root memories makes logical sense.

...letting the subconscious mind lead the way to root memories makes logical sense.

I have two metaphors to describe memory networks to clients: the spaghetti bowl metaphor and the roots metaphor. If the client has already displayed a loose storytelling approach that wanders from one topic to another, I use the spaghetti bowl metaphor. In a giant bowl of spaghetti, you can't tell where a strand starts and ends, and when you pull on one strand, others often come with it. Memory processing is like pulling a thread—any memories attached to that thread (or looped over it) will also naturally come up.

Alternatively, I use the roots metaphor if a client demonstrates a structured and methodical storytelling approach. If each facet of life is a separate garden box - the work box, the marriage box, the family of origin box, etc., each box seems independent, but memories are like Bermuda grass, which has runners that spread, climb, and re-root the plant. We may start at one memory in the work box, but when we pull at it, we discover that it

has a runner that connects to something in a completely
different box.

Some clients feel anxious about the possibility of
discovering "hidden" memories, and I believe that this
is an entirely normal and reasonable fear. It's not unlike
the fear that I had about hypnosis. Regarding "hidden"
memories, I reassure the client that their brain has an
excellent system for isolating distressing memories
behind protective walls. Our goal is not to knock down
the walls but to address the memories already leaking
out and impacting life today. I also remind them that
this is a collaborative process and that we do not need
to proceed until they feel ready. If the experience gets
too scary, we can pause or stop, and they are welcome to
return to their safe/calm space or bring in their spiritual
resources. I also reiterate that I will help them if they feel
stuck at any point in the process. Sometimes, I stop and
pray, asking the Holy Spirit to lead the client's mind only
to memories that will help the client heal.

In selecting EMDR targets, I learned through my negative training experience that a topic that seems "minor"
can be rooted in something significant. Based on that
experience, I do not offer clients the "pick something
small" option. If they fear memory processing, I suggest
a future situation as the first EMDR target. Ideally, the
future scenario is unrelated to past traumas. I try to

focus on something like initiating contact with a new neighbor, staying calm and focused while driving in rush hour traffic, or creating a more efficient morning routine.

I used this approach with my client, "Shana," who sought counseling after being stalked by a former co-worker. During the history taking, she revealed that she lost her dad a few years earlier. At first, Shana would not tell me anything about her relationship with her dad except that they had been very close. She was terrified of needing to think or talk about her dad. She also feared working on the stalking memories because the timeline overlapped with her dad's death.

Rather than focusing on the anxiety, I started her with the future template technique. We targeted Shana's fear of giving a presentation at an upcoming neighborhood meeting. First, I asked Shana what she would need to successfully navigate the scenario. She decided she needed courage. We spent some time having her imagine what courage looks like, when she has been courageous in the past, and who else might "lend" her some of their courage. These memories were reinforced by having her think about how it feels when she is courageous. Then she imagined being in the meeting with that courageous feeling. A few weeks later, she excitedly told me how calm she felt during the presentation.

After that positive outcome from EMDR, she wanted to work on more challenging topics but was still afraid to talk about the memories related to her dad. Since she was still in contemplation on that topic, we completed another future template. Shana shared that it was difficult to recover from the stalking experience because the man might suddenly show up again. The stalker was someone she had worked closely with for a time, and she believed that something was wrong with her because she trusted him. We used "the calm confidence" from her meeting experience as a resource to help her imagine how she wanted to respond if she ever saw the stalker again. After this second target, Shana expressed more confidence in her ability to trust God and her intuition regarding physical safety. At that point, she was ready to process the traumatic stalking memories.

Referring to a list of potential targets is a quick way to identify a new topic when you are unsure what to discuss.

I like to accumulate possible targets during the history taking because it gives me a quick reference point for sessions when the client does not have a problem or topic in mind for that day. It also helps me remember some of the influences that might be at play when working on client-selected targets. In Shana's case, I noted her dad's death as a potential EMDR target, but we never directly targeted memories about her dad.

A few weeks before our last session, Shana spontaneously told me about her dad and how his death left her feeling unprotected. Being stalked just reinforced that feeling. She told me that after processing the stalker memories, she talked to several people about her dad. She discovered that she wanted to think about him and was surprised at how many happy memories had come to mind. Building her confidence for the future and her trust in God gave her the courage to process the past and move out of bereavement.

Identifying problematic memories and patterns is a skill for everyone, not just therapists. Perhaps you have a neighbor who seems bitter about how her life turned out. You may have suggested she seek counseling, but she dismissed your suggestion by saying, "What would that do? It's all in the past." It clearly is not in the past if she keeps retelling the same stories of lament. If you identify a potential target, you can explain how therapy might help. Maybe you want to try counseling but don't know what to discuss. Identifying patterns or stuck places in your story is a great way to start a conversation with a counselor.

The following prompts may help you think through a story (yours or someone else's) and identify potential EMDR targets. If you are doing this exercise for yourself, it may help to write your story or record yourself telling it before using the following exploration process.

What is the story underneath the story?

Listen for minimizing statements such as "It doesn't matter now," "I should have expected that," and "It's not surprising." The critical thing to notice is the dissonance. Imagine a neighbor just spent five minutes complaining to you about her sister-in-law again. Then she says, "Well, whatever, I'm over it." Would you believe her closing statement? Her weekly five-minute rants suggest other-wise. (The dissonance can be the target – the difference between the stated words and emotional and/or physical reactions). In this example, the EMDR target might be "my sister-in-law's condescending smirk." This starting target will probably lead to specific memories that fuel the client's repetitive complaints about her sister-in-law.

What do you notice about the person's energy levels and demeanor during various topics?

When you see someone noticeably deflate, this is an opportunity to ask, "What are you thinking right now about yourself and that situation?" and "How do you wish you could think about yourself despite that situation?" These questions are part of the EMDR-specific target assessment discussed in a later chapter. Still, it is helpful to note this information for the potential target list while the client is accessing the memory network.

What fears do you hear?

What upcoming things are they worried about? I like using future fears as targets because the client already has the disaster scenario in their head and knows what they wish would happen. Using the future template technique often reduces the client's anxiety about the future event and about the EMDR process in general. If, after EMDR, the client handles a situation better than expected, they are more likely to believe that EMDR can help with other topics. It gives you and the client an early "win."

Future scenarios are a good place to start.

How is the person's imagination working against them?

Clients stuck in negative imagination tend to use verbiage that keeps them in a negative perspective, such as "nothing will ever work out for me," "Nothing is sure, so I can't expect God to give me anything good," or "I will never get over this." These types of judgment statements prevent the client from noticing incremental changes. Nothing short of a cataclysmic shift holds credibility for a person stuck in a negative perspective. Negative statements can be EMDR targets, but they are also an opportunity to engage the client in creative or experiential activities.

Metaphors or creative imagery can help move the client out of their assessment and judgment of themselves and the situation or memory. For example, having a client draw themselves as an animal pushes the client into an unfamiliar space where they consider how their various traits match an animal, which means that they are, at least momentarily, interrupted from comparing themselves to other people. Similarly, creating an artistic representation of specific emotions can help the client "look at" the emotion from a different perspective, presenting the option to notice an emotion versus being hijacked by that emotion.

Art therapy activities can also help reveal potential targets. For example, I asked one client to draw a picture of where she is now and her ideal situation. She drew a desert on one side and a bustling city on the other, with a chasm separating the two. Potential EMDR targets were her distress about the current state, dangers about going over to the positive emotional side, and fears that there was no safe path from negative to positive. The beauty of combining art therapy with EMDR is that the client can go back and revise the drawing to illustrate new perspectives or solutions revealed through EMDR processing, so there is a tangible reminder of that shift in perspective or interpretation. Alternatively, the client may create a new drawing and keep the original one to compare then versus now, or a series of drawings if the situation continues to evolve.

Maintaining hope is difficult for clients who are in ongoing situations beyond their control, such as coping with a chronic illness, dealing with a vindictive family member, or navigating a lingering legal battle. In these instances, it is easy for the client to get stuck focusing on the lack of escape routes. The only thing in the client's control is how they choose to interpret the situation. I find it helpful to ask the client, "Do you think it might be possible to feel 'okay' emotionally or spiritually, even if external circumstances stay the same?" This question provides an entry point to explore the concept presented in Philippians 4:7, that God's peace surpasses all understanding. As believers in Jesus Christ, God gives us his Holy Spirit, which means that God's peace is already inside us; therefore, we are capable of experiencing his peace even while enduring suffering and hardship. Sometimes, it helps clients to imagine or draw themselves and God's peace. If the client notices anything separating them from God's peace, that barrier or separation is a good starting target for EMDR.

Perspective may be the only thing in the client's control.

Once you have a draft of potential targets, you can engage the client in a conversation about what you have heard so far, check in on which targets the client is interested in working on, and ask if there are any other memories, patterns, or beliefs that the client would like to add to the list. Then, let the client prioritize. If the client is unsure where to start, I ask if there is an upcoming event that the client is worried or anxious about. If there is a related target memory, we start there. I give anxious clients the choice of starting with the least distressing or most distressing target. It's interesting how often clients choose the most distressing memory because they see it as the fastest path toward feeling better.

CHAPTER EIGHT

ASSESSING THE TARGET

The EMDR assessment phase is the setup for desensitizing a particular memory or body sensation target. We are "assessing" the client's current attitudes, feelings, and body sensations related to a specific target memory, belief, or pattern. A usual memory processing session includes ten to fifteen minutes of target assessment, twenty to thirty minutes of memory work using BLS, and five to ten minutes for session closure. However, these are just guidelines. Every EMDR processing session is different; some progress quickly, some slowly. Some memories stand alone, while others exist within larger patterns with similar experiences. Processing time can differ greatly, even for two people who experience the same event, such as a car accident. One person may process the memory in a single hour. The other person may need several hours to work through all the layers of emotions, resulting experiences, and post-traumatic symptoms. Some therapists routinely schedule double sessions or multi-hour intensive sessions for EMDR memory processing. I primarily offer 50-minute sessions, sometimes necessitating splitting memory processing across multiple sessions. I discuss some of the nuances of that process in Chapter 11.

The EMDR standard protocol specifies a specific order for assessing a target. As a reminder, "memory" refers to the distressing memory the client chose as the EMDR target. The target assessment steps are presented below as questions the therapist asks the client, followed by a brief explanation of the purpose. I hope this will help you imagine the process in action. The underlined words and abbreviations are used for reference later in the chapter.

1. What name would you like to give to the memory? This is the EMDR **Target.**

2. Is there an <u>Image</u> that represents the worst part of the memory? The goal is to help the client fully access the memory network. The image is not necessarily a snapshot of an event; it may represent the primary emotion or belief. For example, if the worst part of a memory was feeling abandoned, the image could be a person huddled alone in a corner. Asking, "What is the worst part of the memory right now?" accomplishes the same purpose.

3. What does this make you believe about yourself? This identifies the **Negative Cognition (NC).** This question confuses some clients. One alternate wording is, "What negative thought do you have about yourself when you think about this memory?" I have noticed that some Christian clients struggle to name a negative belief, perhaps because they have been trained to always look for good in a situation. They tend to start hypothesizing why the other person engaged in hurtful behavior. This pattern often translates in some way to "I should have stopped the other person," "I should have seen it coming," or "I should be over this by now."

4. What positive statement would you like to believe about yourself instead? This identifies a **Positive Cognition (PC)** to replace the NC.

5. How true does that new statement feel? (rate from 1-7, 1= not believable) The **Validity of the Cognition (VOC)** is how true the positive cognition feels to the client. The client may say they know the PC is true but not fully believe it. For example, "I am good enough because God loves me" might be fully valid from a thinking perspective, but emotionally may only feel half-true.

6. What Emotions do you feel right now when you think about the memory? Some clients struggle to identify emotions and default to judgments. For example, the client might say, "I feel like I could have handled that better." I generally seek clarification by offering emotional words in a question such as, "Do you feel guilty, sad, or something else when you say that?"

7. How intense do those emotions feel right now? (rate from 0-10). This is the **Subjective Units of Disturbance (SUD)** rating of the current emotions. The scale is zero to ten. Zero is calm or neutral; ten is the most intense emotion the client has experienced. Some people's stories involve great loss, and the memories will always hold some level of sadness. In those cases, zero may represent "only the appropriate level of sadness" rather than neutral.

8. What Body Sensations do you notice right now? Some clients need additional prompting to report where they feel the emotions in their bodies. It may help to ask, "What part of your body tells you when you have an unpleasant emotion?"

Let's see these steps in action with a client case. Imagine a client comes to talk to you after breaking his wrist. Although the bone is slowly healing, he feels unreasonably impatient and angry with himself. During history taking, you ask if his current situation reminds him of any other memories. He says, "Yes. I broke the same wrist when I was eight years old. I wanted to see inside a bird's nest, so I climbed the tree. I climbed up there okay but lost my balance and fell out of the tree. My mom was so mad at me." You respond, "Well, it makes sense that you might have some extra feelings about that broken wrist. What do you think about trying EMDR to process the memory of falling out of the tree?" If the client agrees, you begin by assessing the target memory. Keeping in mind that most clients are going to give you a lot more detail than necessary, by the end of the conversation, your EMDR assessment notes would look something like this:

Target: *Falling out of the tree*
Image: *being in the ER with mom*
NC: *I should have known better*
PC: *I did the best I could*
VOC: *4 (I'm not totally sure I did my best)*
Emotions: *guilt, sadness, shame*
SUD: *6 (it's a little worse than usual because I'm thinking about it right now)*
Body sensations: *headache, wrist hurts*

The process seems simple enough, but some clients really struggle to answer these questions because they are either too immersed in emotion or unable to access emotion. As it turns out, the standard protocol assessment phase is a bit controversial in the world of EMDR experts. Some experts insist on strict adherence to the specific order of the standard protocol, while others believe that the process interrupts the client's access to the memory.

As mentioned previously, I participated in an EMDR consultation group while pursuing EMDRIA certification. During one of those group meetings, another therapist commented that their client could not identify a positive cognition. She asked our EMDR consultant if it was okay to skip that part of the assessment and return to it later. The consultant told the therapist, "No," because research showed that the particular order of the script was effective. That feedback seemed unhelpful; it communicated that the whole process has to stop if the client cannot access a positive thought or belief.

A few years ago, I faced a similar assessment process dilemma. My client was in high distress, and we were stuck on the positive cognition step. Even with a list of "sample" positive cognitions, she could not identify one that felt accurate. If you recall the discussion about "discombobulated" clients, a person in distress does not have full access to the frontal cortex of their brain. The pre-frontal cortex is where ideas come together; it allows you to notice how you feel while you do a task, and it allows you to change focus and think creatively. Identifying a positive cognition requires creative thinking. How can I expect my client to identify a positive cognition if her creative thinking center is "offline?" Contrary to my consultant's advice, I decided to skip the positive cognition and validity of cognition steps because desensitizing the client's distress seemed more productive than stopping the process until she chose a positive cognition.

I followed my instincts in skipping the positive cognition steps but am not alone in my concerns about the process. Attachment-focused EMDR (AF-EMDR) provides a slightly different science-based rationale for changing the EMDR assessment steps. AF-EDMR explains that the setup for the standard protocol creates problems for some clients because it requires switching back and forth from one side of the brain to the other multiple times. Each brain hemisphere has a unique method of processing information.

The right side of the brain primarily uses symbols, imagery, and metaphor to hold and make sense of input from the emotions and the five physical senses (taste, touch, hearing, sight, and smell). Information in the right hemisphere tends to be clustered together based on similarities. Even if you have never touched a rabbit's fur, you can probably imagine how soft it would feel because your brain stores the concept of fur near your visual memories of "soft" objects and tactile memories of feeling soft, satiny, and smooth objects. A few years ago, I had the opportunity to feed and pet kangaroos and wallabies. I expected the fur to feel like petting a dog and that was true with the wallabies. But I was surprised and delighted when I discovered the kangaroo's fur was much softer, just like petting a rabbit. And now you can store that little tidbit in your "fur" memory network too.

Information in the brain's left hemisphere processes information more linearly using words, logic, and rules. The left brain helps us learn rules through observation. If a child sees the dog pee on the rug and then hears dad say, "bad dog," the child can extrapolate that peeing on the rug is bad, even though that was not explicitly stated. The left hemisphere's job is to help make sense of the world, to create a cohesive story and extract the lesson from each experience.

Switching between sensory and evaluative processes is like trying to do a complex math problem while remembering feeling betrayed by your best friend. They are very different mental tasks. Information processing speed and the ease of switching between tasks vary widely among individuals, but stress often makes both tasks more difficult. With that in mind, let's look at the standard protocol steps again to identify the shifts between sensory and evaluative processes.

Target: *I fell out of the tree/broke my wrist* — This is <u>Sensory</u> , because the client is recalling the sights, sounds, smells, etc. directly connected to the memory.

Image: *being in the ER with my mom* — This is <u>Sensory</u>, focused on the visual input.

NC: *I should have known better* — This may be <u>Sensory or Evaluative</u>. In most cases, the negative cognition is a verbal expression of deeply felt loneliness, failure, or rejection. However, some clients come to the negative cognition based on an evaluative comparison of multiple experiences.

PC: *I did the best I could* — This is <u>Evaluative</u> because the client has to consider the memory in the context of all experiences and decide what additional information might be worth considering.

VOC: *4* — This is <u>Evaluative</u>, because rating on a mathematical scale requires logical comparison.

Emotions: guilt, sadness, shame – This is <u>Sensory</u>, because it moves the client's attention back to their body and emotions.

SUD: *6* — This is <u>Evaluative</u> because it requires comparative logic.

Body sensations: *headache, wrist hurts* — This is <u>Sensory</u> because the client is back to noticing information from the five senses.

This order of assessment steps requires the client to move back and forth between sensory and evaluative modes four times. Since some people struggle to transition quickly from one type of task to the other, the standard protocol may unnecessarily slow the target assessment process.

As someone who struggles with rating scales, I would happily discard the scaling steps. However, I still use the rating scales because it appeals to clients who like evaluative tasks. The rating also helps when the client's body language and facial expressions do not match their emotional state. It occurs with individuals with minimal facial expressions ("flat affect") and clients who smile or tell jokes to hide their distress. I am often surprised at how intensely clients rate their emotional distress when there is little non-verbal indication of intense emotion.

For clients who struggle with evaluative tasks, I often simplify the rating by using category comparisons such as "mild, medium, intense" or "a little true, half true, mostly true." It is also reasonable to reevaluate later in the process by asking if the client's feelings are more intense, less intense, or about the same as the starting point. The main goal is to have a general idea of where the client is starting so you can measure progress later.

EMDR fascinates me because of the spontaneous shifts it produces.

The EMDR process still fascinates me because of the spontaneous shifts it produces. In my experience, well-resourced clients not only downshift in emotional intensity but also often spontaneously develop a PC as they process. My process improvement-minded brain asks, "Why are we wasting time trying to get the client to name a PC during setup if they are likely to develop a completely different PC organically?"

In the last chapter, I mentioned starting with a future template to ease a client into EMDR. There is another benefit to that approach. Successfully processing a future scenario requires the client to imagine using a positive resource. Utilizing a positive resource (in reality or imagined scenario) can also translate into a PC. For example, Shana (from Chapter 7) successfully navigated a presentation after we used a Future Template. Her experience of "staying calm under pressure" became the positive cognition "I can stay calm" for processing fears about encountering her stalker.

Similarly, when processing a past memory, if the emotional distress decreases but the negative belief persists, I may use the future template on the same topic as the target memory. Imagining how a similar future event might unfold distracts the client from regret over past responses and often helps reduce negative sentiment about the target memory. Not every situation lends itself to this type of processing as a resource, but it is a handy tool to keep in mind.

Use Imagination to shift out of negative sentiment.

Theoretically, naming a PC in the setup introduces a new memory network connection, but I am not convinced that this is always necessary, and apparently, AF-EMDR therapists agree. The modified setup offered by AF-EMDR focuses only on the memory and the associated sensory information, omitting the evaluative steps. Let's see how the revised assessment looks, using the example of the client with the broken wrist.

Target: *I fell out of the tree/broke my wrist* — Sensory
Image: *being in the ER with mom* — Sensory
Body sensations: *headache, wrist hurts* — Sensory
Emotions: *guilt, sadness, shame* — Sensory
NC: *I should have known better* — Sensory/Evaluative

The target assessment is simplified to just five steps and requires only one shift from sensory to evaluative focus. This modified assessment makes it simple to transition quickly into the desensitization phase. If the client experienced BLS during the preparation phase, shifting into memory processing is often seamless.

Some of my clients only come to the office for desensitization sessions, so there are times when I need a few extra minutes to prepare the client for the distracting nature of the lightbar and tappers before starting the desensitization phase. The first time the client is in the office, I explain that we can adjust the speed and intensity of the BLS at any time and I verbally predict that it may take a few sets to find the ideal settings. I let them know that the emotion might get more intense during the first set of BLS because we are opening up the memory network, and I remind them to try to observe, not re-live, the target memory. I am not perfect at this process. Sometimes, I forget to state these details and must pause to provide the client with extra guidance and reassurance.

Ideally, the setup phase ends with the client in a state of emotional awareness rather than a logical/evaluative focus. If you had to pause to acclimate the client to the lightbar and tappers or if you needed to make other adjustments, that's okay. You can simply redirect the client's attention to the memory, emotions, and body sensations and then start the desensitization phase.

CHAPTER NINE

DOING
EMDR

Clients sometimes start a session by asking, "Can we do EMDR today?" They are requesting BLS assisted desensitization. They want help turning down the intensity of emotions and sensations. BLS is a central component in the actual processing of a memory. The first step in memory processing is reducing the client's reactivity to the memory. It is the emotional equivalent of learning to play guitar. The first few times you play the guitar, you will likely stop playing after just a few minutes because the strings hurt your fingertips. Repeated exposure through practice desensitizes your fingertips, so the pressure from the strings is no longer a deterrent to playing. Similarly, the mind automatically pulls away from emotionally painful memories. Avoidance works for a time, but desensitization is the healthiest path for true healing and forward progress.

EMDR Desensitization requires observation of multiple sources of input. An EMDR client might describe this process as, "I am watching myself in the memory of an old event AND noticing how I feel now when I think about that event, AND I am noticing that I am physically separate from that event." This process requires the client to stand apart from themselves – it's like watching a movie instead of acting in a play. In most cases, like with guitar practice, each iteration of memory observation makes the pain or sensitivity a little less intense.

BLS aids the desensitization process by helping the client stay aware of their body apart from the memory. EMDR traditionally utilizes eye-movement BLS by having the client look from one side to the other and back in rapid succession. Auditory BLS involves listening to sounds that play in one ear and then the other and back. Tactile BLS includes alternating right and left sensations using buzzers or having the client use their fingers to tap on their shoulders or knees. Thirty-second BLS sets are sufficient for most clients to access the memory without getting overwhelmed by the associated emotions.

As sensitivity decreases, new perspectives and connections can emerge. Sorting experiences and moving new associations into long-term memory usually occurs during REM sleep. BLS provides a means to do that work from a conscious state. Our minds create elaborate networks to group similar things and experiences for more efficient thinking and decision-making. These networks help us examine a restaurant menu and decide which dishes sound appetizing.

Unfortunately, this sorting process sometimes leads to incorrect conclusions. For example, my childhood nemesis was named Erica. Even now, when I meet someone named Erica, I feel defensive. It takes effort for me to engage and get to know this "new" Erica. My mind has generalized the pain from one relationship to all people named Erica.

BLS allows for conscious adjustment of unhelpful generalizations. Shortly after voluntarily changing jobs, "Amy" started experiencing unsettling dreams about people disappearing. During EMDR desensitization of the dreams, Amy explored her sadness and discovered the underlying belief, "Everyone leaves me." Recognizing that it was her choice to change jobs, EMDR desensitization helped differentiate her current sadness from past abandonment memories. Amy chose the PC, "I am setting out on a new adventure," to help maintain that differentiation and reinforce the positive aspects of her recent job change.

Although the purpose of EMDR is not to change memories per se, the reality is that memory networks change every time we access them. Our brains are not dispassionate cameras; we can't help but infuse emotion and meaning into our memories. When we revisit a memory, we either reinforce or weaken our interpretation and the determination of which details are important to remember. Interpretive changes are more likely when we tell the story out loud because we attach the listener's reactions to our understanding of the events. Take, for example, a child who witnesses a crime. The first time the child tells or shows what happened is often the most accurate because the child does not have any adult feedback yet. If an adult responds, "Are you sure that's what happened?" the child may start doubting his ability to recall or evaluate the world around him. He may start believing that he got the story wrong. After a few iterations, he may feel reluctant to tell the story because he no longer trusts his narrative. Similarly, he is also vulnerable to additive suggestion. If a trusted person says, "No, there weren't two people; there were three people," the child may adopt that information into his narrative, effectively changing the memory.

Memory networks change every time we access them.

Most adults are not as sensitive to suggestion, but it is not uncommon for EMDR to cause details of a target memory to become fuzzier or more challenging to recall. Desensitization also lessens the emotional intensity, and like it or not, a dispassionate recalling of events communicates to others that the event really "wasn't all that bad."

Since accuracy and emotion are essential in a crime victim's legal testimony, it is wise to ask about upcoming legal proceedings and delay desensitization of the crime memory until the client's testimony is complete. However, when carefully used, EMDR can help the client imagine having emotion while feeling "collected" enough to talk clearly and coherently in court.

Assuming there is no reason to preserve the details and intensity of a memory, the desensitization process may proceed. The primary concern in this phase is maintaining "dual awareness," which means staying aware of the current counseling space while remembering the distressing event. As mentioned previously, the goal is to observe the memory, not "relive" the experience. Observing the memory creates distance, which helps decrease or even disconnect the intensity of the memory. Emotional intensity often increases during the first BLS set but, in most cases, quickly decreases in subsequent sets.

In my experience, increasing emotional intensity after the second set usually results from me letting the client stay in their silent processing for too long. So, I pay more attention to the client's physical and emotional responses. I let their process inform how I guide the EMDR session, maneuvering myself and the client past fears and roadblocks that might derail the process.

Now that we have discussed the purpose of doing EMDR, the remainder of the chapter is a list of challenges that might stall the therapy process. We will begin with common therapist fears before discussing client fears and hesitations. My hope is that these stories will humanize the internal experiences of both therapist and client and that the Holy Spirit will use these examples to spark creative solutions when you feel stuck or uncertain.

THERAPIST HESITATIONS

"Oh no! My client is completely falling apart!"

I had a client, "Quinn," who experienced severe childhood neglect. When she tried to connect with people outside her family, her mother quickly undermined or severed the client's outside connections. Quinn started therapy more than ten years prior to our first meeting, and saw at least six different clinicians. That set off my "borderline personality disorder" alarm bell.

Clients with borderline personality disorder (BPD) vacillate between intense emotional closeness and hostile distance from other people. They desire close relationships but have a very low tolerance for disagreement or confrontation. They tend to sever ties with people who disagree, challenge their view of the world, or point out issues with their behavioral patterns. BPD clients often bombard their therapist with communications between sessions and engage in emotional manipulations so that sessions go beyond the allotted time. However, if a therapist confronts the client and attempts to reset the boundaries, the BPD client either collapses emotionally or acts as if the therapist is being negligent or neglectful. In the first mode, the client presents like a young child who is inconsolable after being told she is "bad." In the second mode, the client may threaten self-harm or suicide and imply that the client's survival is the therapist's responsibility. Both behavior patterns attempt to manipulate the therapist into "taking care of" the client by returning to the client's preferred emotional proximity. If the therapist is not drawn into the manipulation and holds the client responsible for self-soothing or initiates a psychiatric hospitalization, a BPD client usually retaliates with hostility. Sometimes, the client fires the therapist in a fit of rage. Other times, the therapist ends up exhausted from the manipulation pattern and fires the client (avoiding "client abandonment" claims by providing a list of referrals to other therapists or agencies). Either way, BPD clients often end up with a long list of former therapists.

Quinn certainly demonstrated some of those tendencies. She struggled with endings, often falling apart at the end of each session and requiring another ten to fifteen minutes of my time. However, she generally respected my time between sessions. Her willingness to try to cope on her own between sessions led me to believe that her fear of separation at the end of each session was a trauma response rather than a core aspect of her personality. In any case, I had to go slowly with Quinn because her emotional distress triggered physical pain and panic attacks. Early in our work together, the assessment for a target memory was distressing enough to make her vomit. So, we slowed down and worked on improving her tolerance for emotional distress. I considered abandoning the EMDR process in her case, but I believed that if we could get her body calmed down, memory processing would be helpful.

Shortly after I started working with Quinn, I attended the "EMDR for Chronic Pain" training by Gary Brothers. His process uses bilateral drum beats to trigger the release of GABA (Gamma-aminobutyric acid), a neurotransmitter that helps calm nerve activity associated with pain, fear, and anxiety. Although Quinn did not have chronic physical pain in the traditional sense, I suspected that the bilateral drum tracks would reduce her heightened response to emotional discomfort and the resulting physical pain and panic symptoms.

It turned out that my theory was correct. We paused the discussion each time Quinn started feeling panicky. She listened to the BLS drum track for several minutes until she felt calm enough to continue. I also gave her the homework of listening to the drum track at least once a day. Over time, her tolerance for emotional distress improved, and she successfully engaged in memory processing with the BLS drum track. With most clients, BLS sets are about thirty seconds, but Quinn tended to start re-experiencing her memories within thirty seconds. After a bit of experimentation, we discovered that she could stay in an observational perspective if BLS sets were only fifteen seconds long.

In summary, noting and working with the client's tolerance level helps prevent the client from "falling apart." Clients with a low tolerance for emotional and/or physical pain usually require frequent returns to the preparation phase. It helps to frequently review and celebrate the subtle changes to maintain hope and patience with the process.

Adjusting for the client's tolerance level often helps prevent the client from "falling apart."

"The client is feeling worse! Am I doing this wrong?"

If I see a client getting more visibly upset during the first set, I wonder if they are reliving the memory instead of observing it. If I observe the client crying, their breathing getting more labored, or their brow furrowed, I will cut the first set short to determine if they are reliving or observing the memory. Some clients have trouble staying in observation mode, but icons and metaphors help create emotional distance from a target memory. Interestingly, some people automatically use metaphors, while others require coaching.

One client told me, "The memory got too intense, so I imagined the other person was a bear, and I was up on a cliff looking down at it." This client and others like him inspire me to engage other clients in discussions that encourage creative and imaginative solutions, even when we are not doing EMDR.

When emotional intensity interrupts the client's memory processing, it may take multiple questions and prompts before the client can create symbolism for the people or dynamics in the memory. Once established, I often use the same themes and images with the client as we move into new target memories. In most cases, the imagery becomes vital to how the client integrates memories with current information and understanding.

Metaphors help create emotional distance

For one client, the integration process involved in-teracting with many parts of herself. Some parts were related to specific memories such as "my first day of school" or "the day my baby brother came home." Other parts were connected with specific internal roles, such as "protecting myself." Still, other parts held specific emotions (anger, sadness, confusion). This client imag-ined driving a bus to specific memory settings to rescue stranded parts and sometimes "reclaim the land" by turning a troubling memory landscape into a pleasant memorial space. This client had many difficult childhood memories, so this method of moving through time and "collecting" lost parts of herself was the uniting theme in our work together. It also provided a stable framework to retreat to when processing got stuck or the client felt overwhelmed. Since the client had already described the inner world and how Jesus was integral in keeping her

parts safe and secure, I used her language to help her access that sense of peace at various points.

CLIENT PROCESSING STALLS

"I'm stuck"

Stuck can mean different things in the desensitization phase, but in most circumstances, it refers to the client reaching a point of observing but not knowing what to do next. Feeling stuck may involve seeing oneself trapped or without options in the memory itself. When a client feels trapped in intense emotion, my favorite interweave is to ask whether Jesus is watching the memory with the client. If the client says 'yes,' I invite the client to find out what Jesus is seeing in the memory and what He might like the client to see or know. If the client seems confused, I elaborate, "Imagine Jesus is sitting right next to you while you watch the memory." Following another BLS set, I ask if the client's perspective shifted. Clients commonly see Jesus in the memory scene, providing rescue or defense. Clients also talk about feeling Jesus' comfort in the current moment and reassurance that it is okay to leave the memory in the past.

Clients rarely get stuck in accessing spiritual help, but it happens occasionally. One former client sought counseling because following other people's advice led him into a deeply unsatisfying life. This client's role in his family of origin was "the novice" who never knew what was best for himself. During his childhood, he received so many negative messages about his decisions that he eventually concluded that he could not discern what would be best in his life and could not set a direction for his life without input from others. This helpless perspective led to an unfortunate series of decisions that left him living a life that he did not want and could not extract himself from without causing harm or distress to others.

While we were processing a memory related to childhood abuse, the client got stuck in the fear that he could not accomplish things on his own and that he could not figure out a path forward. Since memory processing had stalled, we started discussing the role of the Holy Spirit in guiding the client. The client visibly relaxed at that idea but still felt skeptical about being able to discern the voice of the Holy Spirit. I asked him to notice the difference between the voice of the Holy Spirit and his family members' voices. And then God did something exciting.

> *I asked him to notice between the voice of the Holy Spirit and his family members' voices. And then God did something exciting!*

During the next BLS set, the client realized that the voice of the Holy Spirit seemed to come from a completely different physical location than the other "advice-givers" in his life. A few sessions later, the client reported that he still felt confused about internal versus external (or spiritual versus physical) messages but had been trying to check in with his body for clarity. This helpful new internal check-in habit emerged from the EMDR session when he received a sense of "direction" regarding the Holy Spirit's voice.

"This seems too easy."

"This seems too easy" is my favorite of all the hesitation responses to EMDR desensitization. The client is experiencing some shift, but their mind is saying, "Wait a second, I've been doing this other routine for years! You can't just expect me to stop at the snap of your fingers. There's no way this can last." I think it's kind of funny and sad because people often want to overcomplicate simple things. People do this all the time with Jesus - they choose not to believe in Him because receiving forgiveness and peace just by believing seems too simple.

They choose not to believe because the solution seems too simple.

Deep inside, the client believes that change must be complex and require much effort and time. Unfortunately, that's a difficult belief to unseat. We get so attached to our suffering and our grudges. We deeply desire a fair and just world, and we want it right now. Yet, if a miracle occurs, we don't trust it. For many clients, it's just a matter of letting life unfold so they can see that the shift is an enduring change for the better. For a client who continues to be anxious about the ease of change, it can be worthwhile to target memories related to the client "taking the easy way out" or family messages about the difficulty of life.

"It's less intense, but I'm still angry, and I don't think the anger will ever go away."

I often hear this from clients who feel wronged by someone else and hold onto their anger because they can't figure out how to "hold the other person responsible." Sometimes, they fear that forgiving will allow the other person to do more damage. Identifying this fear creates an opportunity to explore the difference between forgiveness and reconciliation. It is also an opportunity to remind the client that God's end goal is not for everyone to suffer endlessly. "He does not want anyone to be destroyed, but wants everyone to repent." (2 Peter 3:9). It is not the client's responsibility to make someone else pay or repent. That is the job of the Holy Spirit.

...an opportunity to explore the difference between forgiveness and reconciliation.

Holding a grudge against someone else is unforgiveness, which indicates a client's need for repentance. Why repentance? Repenting is an acknowledgment of error. A client holding onto anger attempts to do the job God identifies as His. "Beloved, never avenge yourselves, but leave it to the wrath of God, for it is written: 'Vengeance is Mine, I will repay,' says the Lord" (Romans 12:19).

When confronted with this perspective and the tried-and-true statement, "Holding a grudge is like drinking poison and hoping that the other person will die," most clients admit that staying angry is exhausting. Harboring anger was mentioned in the "What if the change is bad?" discussion in Chapter 6. Asking the client how much anger or vigilance is minimally necessary to prevent being hurt or deceived in the same way again allows the client to consider releasing excess anger. Inviting the client to visualize the perpetrator under God's judgment may also help the client surrender their rage.

"I am still mad at myself because I should have known better."

Misplaced self-blame is another point for repentance, although many clients won't see it that way immediately. In my experience, most stuck negative cognitions are surface-level cognitions that overlay the belief that "I might be unlovable." Maintaining negative judgment about ourselves is a distraction we use to avoid revealing our unlovability.

Additional work with internal parts of self often helps dismantle negative self-judgments, particularly when a critical perfectionist part is unwilling to accept the naivete of a younger or more vulnerable part. Exploring the needs and motivations of each internal part can lead to more compassion for the self and what was known, unknown, and hidden when the event occurred.

Although unpleasant, being deceived is a common human experience. It is a manifestation of the ongoing battle in the spiritual realm. Satan disguises himself as an angel of light in order to deceive (2 Corinthians 11:13-15) and often uses people to accomplish that goal. It is only through the help of the Holy Spirit that we can discern whether a person is being sincere or setting out to deceive through smooth talk and flattery (Romans 16:18). If we have not been taught what to look for or have not seen it before, how can we "know better" unless the Holy Spirit imparts that knowledge? It is easier to discern whether the guidance is from God's spirit or a deceiving spirit if we regularly study the Bible and pray, but we all get deceived. That's just part of being human.

"I can't look at it/I can't think about it."

Many clients are reluctant to process a memory because they imagine it will be too painful to think about the memory. This moment of hesitation is a great time to instruct the client about the purpose of dual awareness, to remember that they are here in the session and can observe the memory without reliving it. Keeping their eyes open or using eye movements rather than tactile or audio BLS often helps the client maintain dual awareness.

When clients are too fearful to watch the memory, I use a containment technique. I ask the client to imagine that the memory is a movie file saved on a computer. They don't have to run the movie; they can focus on the file icon instead. Some clients imagine the file on the computer desktop; others bury the file in several layers of folders, completely hidden from view. Once that process is fully imagined, I revisit the assessment by asking, "What does the existence of that memory file say about you?" This question often accesses core identity beliefs such as "I'm defective" or "I'm ruined." If the negative cognition shifts, I update the remainder of the assessment before resuming desensitization. Clients who experience intrusive and overwhelming memories

often feel relieved when the memory can be closed, put away, or set at a distance.

Clients often feel relieved when the memory can be closed, put away, or set at a distance.

Ron, who was mentioned in Chapter 6, had obsessive-compulsive disorder (OCD), which made it difficult for him to hold onto hopeful or optimistic beliefs. Part of the OCD was a fear that bad memories would taint good memories, so it was necessary to create imagined barriers to prevent the risk of the memory touching or tainting anything good in the current moment. It took us the better part of a therapy session to devise the solution that finally worked for Ron: to imagine that the memory was on a TV and the TV was on a faraway mountain. Hence, he had to look through binoculars to watch the

memory. It took three levels of containment for him to start processing the bad memory.

Another option for the "I can't think about it" scenario is to use the fear of memory processing as the first target. Targeting the fear is like metacommunication, which is "communication about communication" or "talking about talking."

Early in my counseling career, I met with a young boy who was grieving the unexpected death of his father. His mother was in the room with us, and despite her encouragement, he was utterly unwilling to talk about his dad's death. I suspected that he was trying to protect his mother, so we talked about what might happen if he were to talk about his dad's death. In that metacommunication process, he eventually relaxed and started talking about his dad and how he died. It turned into a beautiful moment of shared grief with his mother.

I have seen a similar process happen with EMDR when targeting the fear of processing turns into actual memory processing. The fact that the clients move from the fear of processing into actual processing proves that EMDR works. Desensitizing the fear allows a client to view the memory differently.

"I'm afraid to talk about it."

It is important to clarify if the client distinguishes between "I'm afraid to talk about it" versus "I can't think about it." Sometimes, the client is okay thinking about the memory but fears traumatizing the therapist. Clients with military or law enforcement backgrounds often demonstrate this desire to protect the therapist. When fear for the therapist is the real issue, I give the client permission to process without sharing details. "Blind processing" can be complex for the therapist. Our natural inclination is to ask for more information, and we use those details to help us stay oriented to the client's mental and emotional state.

Sometimes the client wants to protect the therapist.

The usual post-set question is, "What are you noticing now?" which clients usually interpret as, "What did you see or imagine?" In blind processing, a better question is, "What is happening now with your thoughts, feelings, and body sensations?" This question helps remind both therapist and client that the goal is to desensitize, not to describe the scene.

You might be wondering, "But how do I know if the client is staying on track?" One option is to ask, "Were you able to stay with the memory, or did your mind take you somewhere else?" If the mind took the client elsewhere, then ask "does that feel related or does it feel like an escape from the memory?" In this way, you can tell if the client is running into internal fear or resistance that might necessitate a return to preparation. Another option is to prompt the client to focus on the target memory again after every two or three sets.

"I'm worried about what that person thinks about me right now."

Working on memories related to a person still involved in the client's life can be difficult, particularly if the client is still feeling criticized, marginalized, or manipulated by that person. Often, this issue presents itself as the client jumping from an earlier memory into a more recent interaction. In those cases, I treat it as a related memory and ask the client to return to the target memory to continue processing.

It can be difficult to work on memories about a person still in the client's life.

Suppose the same more current memory comes up again. In that case, I might ask what was different about that recent event. Usually, once the client can see and state the difference between past events and the current situation, the client can resume working on the target memory.

One client had this dynamic show up in a very unusual way. The client was working on memories of her mother but kept having the intrusive sensation that her mother was standing over her shoulder and criticizing the client for needing therapy. I asked the client what she would like to do with that "hovering mother." The client imagined moving her mother to a different place in the room to remove that sense of hovering criticism.

The client then decided that was insufficient and proceeded to create an imaginary room behind me and asked Jesus to send an angel to guard that door so her mother could not barge in again. This moment was an opportunity to utilize the "defender" figures established during the "internal support team" exercise, as discussed in chapter 6. Once the "hovering mother" was securely in that imagined room, the client continued working on the target memory.

"I don't know if I am doing this right."

It is surprising how often clients fixate on trying to be perfect in the processing phase. They get confused about where to focus, what to do while concentrating, and whether the goal is to change the memory. When a client says, "I'm not sure if I'm doing this right," I usually ask, "Well, what happened during the set?" In most cases, it's not that anything "wrong" happened during the set; it's more that the client just felt anxious because they are used to having to "do" something rather than sit and observe.

When a client says they "popped out" of the memory, this usually indicates that the emotional intensity got too intense. For "popping out" situations, my first question is, "Were you watching the memory, or did you get pulled into reliving the event"? It is almost always the latter. The client needs reminding that the goal is not to relive but to look at the scene and see what they notice. It sometimes helps to invite the client to focus on one image instead of trying to watch the memory like a movie.

If the client reports that they had the memory in mind, but as soon as the BLS started, they could not access the memory, I will normalize that the BLS can have that effect and ask them to try again now that they know what to expect. If the issue continues, I slow down the BLS or reduce the intensity of the buzzers so the mind is less distracted by the BLS. If the client cannot stay focused on the memory after several sets, I remind them that everyone is a little different, and it often takes time for me to figure out what works best for a client. I might even thank the client for bearing with me, essentially pulling the responsibility for the process onto myself to reduce the client's anxiety. When new fears and worries surface during memory processing, it is okay, perhaps even advisable, to revisit the client's internal meeting space to address questions and concerns. Resolving the client's ambivalence and anxieties may increase their ability to stay focused on the memory during BLS.

Some clients just can't stay with an image during BLS even with all the other adjustments, and, in many cases, processing still occurs. In my experience, once the client recalls the sensory aspects of a particular memory, that memory can be desensitized even if the client's attention shifts during a BLS set. For example, let's say I just completed a target assessment, and the client reported a distress level of seven. As I hand the BLS tappers to the client, I realize we have not yet completed the "safe place" activity. So, we pause and use BLS to help the client access a calm state with the "safe place" in mind. To refocus on the desensitization phase, I read aloud the information target assessment when the client interrupts to say that her level of distress is only a five now. Although unintentional, some memory desensitization occurred during the "safe place" BLS sets. This experience tells me that maintaining focus on the image during BLS sets is not critical for desensitization. If the client can access the memory between sets and reports decreasing distress, keep going. If the client's distress level is not decreasing, you may need to look for blocking beliefs (as discussed at the end of Chapter 6).

"What if I am not remembering the details or I'm making things up?"

It is tempting for the client to believe that if they don't remember specific details, they can't heal from the experience. This concern is common for clients with fragmented memories. It is easy for the therapist to forget that EMDR is not about remembering all the details of the memory; it's about reducing ongoing distress by addressing unhelpful meanings associated with the memory. When a client seems stuck trying to remember, I either direct their attention back to their general feelings about the memory or ask what makes them believe it might be essential to remember a particular detail. The client's fixation on remembering details is a blocking belief. Blocking beliefs can be treated as interim targets within target memory processing. I usually just put a star in my notes to mark the detour in the desensitization process.

For clients concerned about the future effects of memory processing, the fear of making up details can be a huge concern. I recall one client "Beth," who worried about the accuracy of her memory because she thought that she would have to confront the person who abused her.

When I asked her why she would have to confront the abuser, she said, "I thought that's what I am supposed to do." "Really," I asked, "who told you that?" Beth did not have an answer to that question, so we paused EMDR to explore the pros and cons of confrontation.

"Really? Who told you that?"

The client relaxed as our conversation revealed new options. We resumed the EMDR processing, and by the end of the session, Beth was no longer concerned about future interactions with the perpetrator. When I asked for more details, she said she did not need to confront that person, but if the situation arose, she could handle it. I find it interesting that we did not actively work on her ability to interact calmly with the abuser. Yet, Beth's creative, prediction-generating mind provided a calm and confident option for that future scenario.

Desensitization of emotional reactions is just the first step in processing memories. The goal of memory processing (whether through normal sleep processes or EMDR therapy) is to use experiences to help us understand who we are and how the world works.

If we stop after desensitization, the client won't get the full benefit of EMDR. For example, if a client's memory of failing a college class has been desensitized but not fully processed, he can think about the experience without anger but still believes the NC, "I'm a dumb jock." I don't want to leave my client in a state of hopelessness. I want my client to be brave enough to pursue his dream, even if he gets knocked down a few times. The cognition, "I'm just a dumb jock," predicts failure, but I want my client to decide between trade school and college based on his interests and abilities, not based on a pessimistic prediction that may be inaccurate. So, in the interest of helping people pursue their life dreams, let's move on to the next phase: Installation of the positive cognition.

CHAPTER TEN

INSTALLING
THE GOOD

Installation is the phase for attaching a positive cognition to the target memory. The goal is to make the memory a usable experience rather than something to be feared or avoided. There are various degrees of positivity. For example, strong positives are "God helped me through it" and "I am stronger now." If a client sees nothing valuable or redeemable about a memory, the positive cognition might be a neutral statement such as "It's over now" or "I escaped." Many of my clients naturally shift into the installation phase without explicit prompting. Beth (the client from the end of Chapter 9) reported that if she encountered the person who abused her, she could handle it. "I can handle it" was her spontaneously generated positive cognition.

A positive cognition that comes up spontaneously is the more powerful statement because it comes from a place already connected to the memory network. If a Christian client's positive cognition does not explicitly mention God, Jesus, or the Holy Spirit, I may ask how the PC fits with their understanding of God's role in their situation. This question sometimes prompts the client to revise the PC, and in most cases, adding spiritual help or perspective seems to create a more profound sense of calm. I usually do one or two more BLS sets and then move on because I think it is more valuable to move into future scenarios where the PC can be "tested."

A positive cognition that comes up spontaneously is more powerful...

If Beth had expressed concern about encountering her abuser, we could have used the Future Template technique (mentioned in Chapter 7) to have her imagine handling the situation well. The Future Template helps generalize the new positive cognition and creativity to other similar situations. I like to have the client use self-tapping (tapping on the shoulders or knees) for this process because it reminds them that they can do this for themselves as needed outside of the therapy room.

If the client imagines a negative outcome during the future template, we pause and discuss what feels distressing, I remind the client of the positive cognition, and then begin another BLS set. In most cases, the client can visualize a consistently "calm" response to a future scenario by the third set.

If the anxiety persists, the Flash Forward technique is a good alternative. The Flash Forward starts with assessing the future scenario and proceeds through desensitization and installation, just like any other target. After completing the Flash Forward, resume installation for the original target. In most cases, this resolves any block in the validity of the positive cognition.

Some clients get nervous because although the future scenario imagining went well, they fear they might not be able to act as they wish when the event occurs. In these cases, I brainstorm with the client about how they can remember that there is a new way to respond.

In *For Love of the Game*, Kevin Costner's character Billy Chapel uses the phrase, "clear the mechanism." This phrase was his conscious handle for tuning out distractions and reaching a mental space of calm while pitching. This type of "handle" can provide a quick way of accessing a calmer physical state, which increases the likelihood of productive problem-solving and measured responses in chaotic situations. Some people will choose a word or phrase, but others will choose an object as a reminder of this new calm state of being. Physical handles are a particularly beneficial tool for anxious clients. Many people choose a memento they can wear or carry with them such as a bracelet or a special coin. One of my clients hung a photograph of a lighthouse in his office to remind him to stop and breathe.

The installation phase tends to differ between Christian and non-Christian clients. While the installation phase is essential because it introduces a new neutral or positive cognition into the memory network, there is an opportunity to create a spiritual monument when God is involved. For example, the lighthouse photo chosen as a calming reminder was also a spiritual monument. At several points in the past, the client sat on the beach near

that lighthouse, seeking God's guidance for major life decisions. It was a location where he felt God's presence.

The concept of spiritual monuments derives from several stories in the Bible where people encountered God and then marked a geographical point as a memorial for the encounter. Reminders of these kinds of moments were usually piles of rocks, but for the modern world, it might be a mug, photograph, ticket stub, or even a physical scar or tattoo.

You must be very careful not to forget the things you have seen God do for you. Keep reminding yourselves, and tell your children and grandchildren as well. Deuteronomy 4:9 (CEV)

In general, a spiritual monument accomplishes several things. It is a reminder of specific encounters with God and how God provided. It also acknowledges God's authority and prompts renewed trust in God for peace, rest, and wisdom.

In Genesis chapter 16, Sarai's slave, Hagar, runs away because she was being mistreated after becoming pregnant. While Hagar was in the wilderness near a well, God spoke to her, telling her to return to Sarai's household and revealing His plans for Hagar's son. As a slave, Hagar was probably used to being invisible in many settings. The fact that God not only saw her but had plans for her future was significant enough for her to name the well "beer-lahai-roi" which means "the well of the living One who sees me." This became her spiritual monument of how God reassured her and gave her the courage to return home.

As demonstrated in Hagar's story, spiritual monuments are often preceded by some form of struggle. This was true for my client "Adam" who sought counseling shortly after his wife left him. We worked together for several years, helping him come to terms with his abusive behavior toward his wife and processing childhood memories of neglect, abuse, and abandonment. We used both EMDR and internal parts discussions to process his anger toward his wife. Anger shifted into horror at his past behaviors, horror turned to compassion for his wife, and compassion compelled him to stop aggressively pursuing her. He had come a long way but was plagued by feeling unlovable.

As we explored his abusive patterns, Adam realized that feeling unlovable was fueling his anger and manipulative behaviors, which made it difficult for people to love him. Adam also realized that if he wanted to change, he needed God's help. He needed comfort from God instead of idolizing validation from other people. Because of the persistent unlovable feelings, we started processing early childhood memories. Unlike earlier EMDR sessions, Adam began experiencing vivid metaphorical imagery indicating spiritual warfare. At one point, he saw a glass wall hiding something. When a handle appeared, Adam opened the door and discovered "abuse" and darkness. Other images included a dragon raining down fire and an animated illustration-style scene of demons entering him as Jesus left. Adam also saw comforting spiritual images, like Jesus tucking him into bed, stroking his hair, and telling him he was lovable.

The "spiritual breakthrough" session occurred about eighteen months into the therapy. During that session, Adam saw Jesus reach through a window to rescue him from a dark room. Then he was taken to a party. Although Adam felt excited about the party, he feared he did not belong there. A few sets later, Adam saw his father berating him, but another figure was in the scene. The figure removed Adam from his father's anger, taking him to another party where multiple people hugged him in greeting. This time, Adam reported feeling safe, loved, and happy.

The various images of Jesus rescuing him serve as spiritual monuments, reminding Adam that he is loved and secure in Jesus' care. Although we continued working together for another year, Adam used more hopeful language after that session and seemed less hesitant about making significant positive changes in his life.

In my personal therapy experience, my counselor assigned me the homework of creating a theme park or similar fun and safe place for my younger self. Interestingly, I needed prompting to engage in the same imaginal activity that occurred spontaneously for Adam when he connected with Jesus.

I frequently remind myself that counseling is God's work, which He allows me to facilitate. Adam's story is just one example of that reality. As positive cognitions settle into our bodies and we allow ourselves to receive God's care and direction, embracing hope and leaving the pain in the past becomes easier.

CHAPTER ELEVEN

LEAVING
THE PAIN IN
THE PAST

The final steps of the EMDR process are the body scan, closure, and re-evaluation. Body Scan and Closure generally happen in the session's last five to ten minutes, and re-evaluation occurs at a follow-up meeting. The body scan at this point is often uneventful because I ask clients about their body sensations throughout the EMDR process, and sometimes the body sensation is the target. However, I still value the body scan phase because disagreement between body sensations and the installed positive cognition indicates that memory processing is incomplete.

There is a link between body sensations and thoughts. For example, if I think, "I am tense," I might unconsciously tighten my neck and shoulder muscles, bracing for a fight. The reciprocal relationship also exists; if I consciously relax my shoulders, my thoughts usually change to "I am less tense" or "I am relaxed." Since humans learn through experience before adding language, physical body sensation messages often trump opposing thoughts. Consider listening to a neighbor talking about her new job. She uses a chirpy tone to tell you, "It's great," but there's a wobble in her voice; she's not smiling with her eyes and has her arms crossed. While part of you wants to believe her words, another part wonders why she does not look happy or excited. The information you receive from the neighbor's non-verbal communication makes you doubt the veracity of her words.

Body messages often trump opposing thoughts.

The same thing happens inside of each one of us. You might say, "I'm over it; let's go do something fun!" However, if there's still a pit in your stomach and a tight feeling in your throat, some part of you is not convinced that it is okay to relax and move on with life. It is tough to truly leave pain in the past if part of you is still constantly bracing for danger. The EMDR Body Scan phase solidifies positive shifts through congruence between body and mind. In most cases, when a client focuses on any remaining tension connected with the target, the sensations quickly diminish. When the tension persists, earlier spiritual visualizations can help clients find peace in their bodies as they focus on God's attentive love.

Visualizing being in God's care can bring peaceful feelings.

Although closure always occurs after the body scan, closure may also occur in the middle of memory processing. The goal of the closure phase is to help bring the client to a place of readiness to re-enter regular life. Regardless of where you pause in the memory processing, a containment activity is advisable at the end of each session. Containment activities help the client "put away" a memory or close a memory network to prevent undue distress between sessions. Since most of my clients process ongoing rather than discreet memories, I often ask the client if there is anything that feels emotionally charged they would like to put away or leave in God's care.

While I don't have any particular "amazing" stories to share about containment, it has been interesting to hear the variations of how clients visualize this process. Some are very straightforward in following the guidance to put the memory into a container. Others decide to leave the box at the foot of the cross. Putting the other person in God's lap is a helpful alternative if the client feels weird about putting other people into a container. After containment, I usually ask the client if I may pray for them before they leave. If they say 'no,' I will ask if they want to end with a calming visualization instead. Either way, the client gets a final moment of peace or calm focus before leaving the session.

My favorite example of closure was with a client who had a processing style that was very different from most. We tried the standard protocol a few times, but she immediately shifted into metaphors and insisted on narrating what was happening rather than silently noticing. Although contrary to the standard protocol trainings. She was good at maintaining an observational state (rather than reliving painful moments), and she told me everything as it happened so I had insight into her process. I decided to stop the power struggle and let her process in her unique way. We settled into a routine of her narrating while the BLS ran continuously. I took notes while she narrated, asking a question here and there when she seemed stuck.

We were close to the end of processing one particular memory, and although the memory did not feel distressing anymore, the client felt that she needed to close that chapter of her life. I invited her to imagine closing that chapter. The client reported imagining herself in a hallway and trying to close the door to the past. She was frustrated because each time she reached toward the door, it seemed to move away from her. I prompted her to ask God for help with the door. She was silent for a few moments, and then her eyes popped open, and she said, "God told me to ask you to help me." It was a moment of minor panic for me as I thought, "What? Why would God tell you that? How should I know?" In all our previous sessions, the client had come to a resolution directly through her interactions with God. Seeking my input was an odd break from that pattern. Maybe that's why I believed her rather than prompting her to ask God again. Thankfully, I didn't share my panic with the client. I paused momentarily and asked the first question that came into my mind.

I asked, "Are you facing the door?" She closed her eyes as she re-entered the imagined scene and answered, "Yes."

"And when you reach for it, the door moves away from you?" I asked.

"Yes."

"Okay, What happens if you face the other direction?" I asked.

She said, "That seems okay. The door is right behind me now."

I paused, unsure what to do with this information. Eventually, I asked, "Can you reach behind you and close the door without looking back at it?"

"Yes! That worked!" She said.

It was a fun moment of success and celebration. We marveled at the solution. She could finally leave that pain in the past. I must credit the Holy Spirit for that creative solution to this client's metaphor. I still wonder why He even prompted the client to ask me for a solution when God usually gave her answers directly. Perhaps it was His kindness, knowing I would return someday looking for spiritual monuments.

CHAPTER TWELVE

BEAUTY
FROM
ASHES

E MDR literally changes your mind, not in the sense
of manipulation, but in the sense of transformation
and expanding understanding. It's one embodiment of
Romans 12:2, "Do not be conformed to this world, but
be transformed by the renewal of your mind, that by
testing you may discern what is the will of God, what is
good and acceptable and perfect." Positive shifts often
occur on the day of memory processing, but in some
cases, the re-evaluation phase reveals more fundamental
changes. The re-evaluation phase occurs at the

beginning of the client's next session unless the client has reason to contact me between sessions. Re-evaluation explores positive shifts from the last session and assesses whether the target is fully processed.

It still surprises me that many clients do not think about the EMDR target between sessions. Some clients even forget that they worked on a particular memory. This forgetfulness indicates that the memory was either properly contained or successfully processed. Some clients need assistance re-containing distressing thoughts or feelings between sessions, but most people continue life as usual. I feel amused when a client returns with a story from the past week about how they responded to a situation with much less anger or distress than usual, yet they do not attribute the shift to the EMDR work. As their therapist, I often see a direct correlation between EMDR processing and the client's behavior change. But in many cases, the client will say something like, "I just got over it, I guess." That's a transformed mind.

Some clients forget that they processed a particular memory.

I want to close this story with a few happy endings. While there have been many successes, these three stories illustrate the spectrum of possible reactions and outcomes from re-evaluation.

Sometimes change is quicker than you expect

One of my recent clients sought counseling because she wanted to quit smoking. She had quit previously but was finding it difficult to stop this time. We chose the most recent cigarette craving as the target memory to help the client understand the nuances of that craving and what emotion she was trying to assuage. The client started thinking about her other self-soothing options a few minutes into the EMDR desensitization phase. Since she had already moved to the installation of positive coping techniques, we shifted to a future focus. I had her imagine the next expected craving. After the first future-focused set, she mentioned a recent experience of calming herself by taking deep breaths because smoking was not an option in that location. I reframed the cigarette cravings as a craving for more oxygen. From that perspective, the cigarettes are a tool for her to breathe deeply. I invited her to consider replacing the crutch of cigarettes with something different. I do not recall what she came up with, but she seemed happy with the solution.

When we met again the next week, she reported that she had not smoked a cigarette since the previous session. In that week, she had only noticed a craving once and was able to soothe her anxiety using the technique from the processing session. Part of me was surprised by her immediate success, but in retrospect, it makes sense. The "non-smoking" memory network was already there; she just needed a new bridge to access it.

Sometimes more work is required

On the opposite extreme, I had a client who reported that she still felt emotionally oppressed after several EMDR desensitization sessions. Any remaining intensity around a memory indicates a need to either revisit the target or change the target slightly to address a new aspect of the memory network.

I found this client's situation interesting because we had desensitized multiple memories of teenage conflicts with her brother, but the general topic still agitated the client. The client's usual desensitization process had a pattern that started with anxiety, then tears, then calm, and then metaphor during the installation phase.

This time, the client went straight into a metaphorical image. She was standing on the shore of a pond facing her brother, looking at the lily pads and wondering whether they were sturdy enough to hold her up.

In the next round, she realized she could go in other directions and that the lily pads were not the only path forward. She also shifted her stance so her brother was at her side instead of straight ahead.

Since their sibling relationship was more collaborative as adults, the metaphorical change in stance was a way of accepting, or perhaps embracing, this new normal. She might have struggled to embrace that collaborative shift if we had not completed the re-evaluation. This example beautifully illustrates the goal of leaving the past in the past and fully embracing the new reality.

Sometimes God is doing spiritual surgery

Sometimes, God is doing much more profound work than we might imagine. I worked with one remarkable woman who was strong in body and mind, but she was exceedingly weary. Her husband suffered an injury on the job, and previous friends and allies were either unwilling to help or actively worked against them as they sought justice and compensation for his medical care. She was essentially doing multiple full-time jobs as she struggled to keep the family above water emotionally, physically, and financially. It was a dark time in many ways, and the client repeatedly commented that she felt violated.

"Violated" seemed like an odd descriptor for the current events, which made me suspect that earlier memories were interfering. I used the "being violated" feeling as the primary target for EMDR. One of the client's associations with this feeling was a childhood memory when she felt responsible for her father's violent behavior toward her and others. While processing that memory, the client received imagery of the spiritual realm during the event, specifically the presence of demons in her house. During the next BLS set, the client reported that she saw angels of protection, and in the subsequent set, she described a separation and a "tearing away" from the darkness. Once that imagery concluded, the client reported that the memory felt like it happened a lifetime ago.

The memory felt like it happened a lifetime ago.

At the next session, when I asked if anything else had come up from the EMDR processing, the client reported that it felt like she had undergone surgery. She quickly followed up with reassurance that the memory processing led to a significant shift in her sense of self. She had been distressed because she felt blindsided by all the betrayals relating to her husband's injury. After processing, she felt confident that she would receive spiritual help to identify unsafe people. Things changed in a very positive direction for the client and her family just a few months later. This was "beauty from ashes."

The Spirit of the Sovereign Lord is on
me, because the Lord has anointed me to
proclaim good news to the poor.

He has sent me to bind up the
brokenhearted, to proclaim freedom for the
captives and release from darkness for the
prisoners, to proclaim the year of the Lord's
favor and the day of vengeance of our God,
to comfort all who mourn, and provide for
those who grieve in Zion— to bestow on
them a crown of beauty instead of ashes,
the oil of joy instead of mourning, and a
garment of praise instead of a spirit of
despair.

They will be called oaks of righteousness, a
planting of the Lord for the display of his
splendor.

Isaiah 61:1-3

CHAPTER THIRTEEN

BE STRONG
AND
COURAGEOUS

So much freedom and beauty are possible when people join with God's creative spirit during EMDR therapy. Fear is the biggest threat to therapeutic success. Fear causes avoidance on both sides of the therapy room; clients hold back or don't show up, and therapists stick with what feels safe and comfortable for both parties. It takes great courage to overcome all the fears — fears of pain, fears of failure, fears of judgment, fears of causing harm. The amazing thing is that God knows this about us. There are more than thirty verses in the Bible where God tells people not to fear but to be strong and courageous. Easier said than done. But the Bible gives us additional instructions on how to be courageous. It reminds us over and over again that God is with us, guiding us, sheltering us, protecting us, defending us, and helping us. It tells us that God's "perfect love casts out fear" (1 John 4:18).

As clients, embracing that perfect love means choosing to trust that God wants to heal us, even when we don't understand the process or timing. Jesus does not want to cause us pain, although we may feel pain as our Great Physician cleans and disinfects our emotional and spiritual wounds. But there's more: He does not start the healing process and then walk away. He stays close by, offering comfort but not forcing it upon us.

As therapists, embracing perfect love means balancing between empathy and sympathy. Our empathy is both a strength and a vulnerability. Empathy lets us connect deeply with another person, but it activates the part of our mind that remembers fear and pain. It is hard to be courageous in a state of empathy, but it's challenging to be creative when simply following a script. We must step back to a place of sympathy, where we understand the client's experience without feeling all the pain and fear within our minds.

Perfect love allows us to find a balance between our responsibilities and God's responsibilities. We need courage to step into uncomfortable client stories without shrinking back or rushing the client through the process. Sticking to the script without discernment limits our ability to be helpful. Perfect love reminds us that we are assistants in God's healing work. As we focus on God and listen for the Holy Spirit's guidance, that quiet voice will guide our work by imparting wisdom, knowledge, and creativity. We can trust Him to guide the process.

When we let God guide our lives, we must manage our fear of disappointing or angering other people. Private practice therapists, in particular, live in a precarious place where our ability to "make people happy" impacts our professional reputation and the flow of new referrals. It often seems that our clients (or potential clients) hold complete power over our careers, financial stability, and long-term security. But God is our true provider. Our job is not to make everyone happy; our job is to listen to God and go where he leads us. Although counseling may be part of your life's mission, it is unlikely to be your only calling. If God has called you to counsel, He will equip you and open doors that only He can open.

I encourage you to consider where you are fearful. Where are you striving to accomplish things through your own power? Are you unwilling or unable to cope with rejection? Your fear is a deterrent to clients and your disobedience hinders God's creative flow.

Running a private practice was not my dream; it was an act of obedience. I told God early on, "Okay, I'll do this, but you know I don't want to, and if it's going to work, you have to provide the clients." He did just that, and I enjoyed running the business after I settled into the process. As I write this (almost 15 years later), the business is declining. I am waiting for God to clarify whether He is ending or pausing my private practice calling. During the first few months of declining business, I was worried and fearful. I did everything in my power to slow the business decline, to publicize the practice, and to get people to say 'yes' to counseling. Eventually, I realized that my striving was fruitless. Then I remembered prior times when I was afraid of losing clients, let pride take over, or simply forgot that the business belongs to God. Every time I tried to take control, God withdrew his support. I looked for where I might be at odds with God, thinking that God might be disciplining me again. But, as I reflected on the situation, I realized that this situation was different. My interest in running the practice has waned while my interest in artistic activities grows brighter every day. God is leading me in a new direction.

I do not know where God is leading you, but I do know He is pursuing you. He has tailor-made opportunities for you if you choose to follow Him. Be brave and courageous. God has a pattern of equipping the least likely candidates. Your insecurity is not a disqualification. Lean into him, listen, and use your creativity to express your awe and wonder. "Oh, taste and see that the Lord is good! Blessed is the man who takes refuge in him!" Psalm 34:8.

To my fellow therapists: I pray blessings on you, I pray that God will deepen your hunger for Him and your personal relationship with Jesus, and I pray that the Holy Spirit will infuse your counseling work with beautiful and awe-inspiring moments of creativity and transformation so that you too can recognize your spiritual monuments.

To those on the healing journey with Jesus: Take heart; joy comes in the morning! The beauty of "the valley of the shadow of death" is that it's just a shadow. That shadow cannot exist without God's light nearby. He is close to you. Reach out, call out; Jesus is listening. Your journey is a witness of God's love and presence.

To those who are here out of curiosity or care for others: thank you for being here. Witnessing is important. I pray that this book has provided understanding. I pray that you will go boldly and share what you have learned. I pray that God will season your words with love as you encourage others to seek help. The world needs people willing to escort others to the doorstep of healing.

To those on the doorstep: Come in. Freedom is here. Healing is here. Call on the name of Jesus, and he will provide you with the courage you need to cross the threshold. I pray that your desire to be well will outweigh your fear of the pain. God cares deeply for the brokenhearted, and that includes you.

I thank you sincerely for joining me on this journey.

In Christ's love,
Angela

Join me in spreading the news;
together let's get the word out.

God met me more than halfway,
he freed me from my anxious fears.
Look at him; give him your warmest
smile.

Never hide your feelings from him.
When I was desperate, I called out,
and God got me out of a tight spot.

God's angel sets up a circle
of protection around us while we
pray.

Open your mouth and taste, open
your eyes and see— how good God is.
Blessed are you who run to him.

Psalm 34:3-8 MSG

STIRRING CREATIVITY

Ultimately, all of my examples won't do you any good unless you also create a space for your creativity, intuition, and connection with the Holy Spirit. Setting aside unstructured and undistracted time to connect to self and God can be challenging. I'm right there with you. I spent two weeks avoiding writing because I felt afraid. What is worse is that, instead of letting myself sit with that discomfort to see how God would lead me through it, I filled my time with mindless activities that in no way benefited me or anyone else.

I once read about an author who got so frustrated with his procrastination that he smashed his modem to force himself to focus on his creative process instead of distracting himself with other people's stories. I was almost ready to smash my iPad for the same reason, but God gave me an extra dose of self-control to get the writing back on track. Hopefully, you are turning to God rather than toward the hammer to break through your avoidance and procrastination. Let's shift away from thinking about other people and use this chapter to focus on cultivating your creativity.

Repeating a process reinforces the neurons connected to that task. The goal of this activity it to access and expand your creative neural network. The easiest place to start is by remembering. Consider the concept of "neurons that fire together wire together." That means that the things that you do, while you remember, will be added to that memory network. So, be deliberate with your time and attention. The Bible verse for this process is Philippians 4:8 (CEV), "Finally, my friends, keep your minds on whatever is true, pure, right, holy, friendly, and proper. Don't ever stop thinking about what is truly worthwhile and worthy of praise." This is not the time to beat yourself up for all your creative failures. It is a time to revel in how it felt during your playful and creative successes and to imagine ways you can bring some of that joy and wonder into today's experiences.

Take your time with the first activity. Consider coming back to this activity daily for a week. If you have a photo of yourself as a child, look at that photo and think back to how you utilized your imagination at that time. Feel free to copy these pages if you don't want to write in your book.

My favorite toys
_____
My favorite games
_____
My favorite art supplies
_____
My favorite dance style
_____
Toys I made
_____
Things I built
_____
Things I took apart
_____
Stories I wrote/told
_____
Songs I made up
_____
Things I used to make
_____
Games I invented
_____
Things I re-purposed
_____
Things I pretended
_____
Things I drew
_____
Things I sculpted
_____
Things I made with food
_____
My craziest experiment
_____

_____

_____

_____

_____

_____

Having trouble getting started on this activity?
The next page has a few more specific prompts.

Did you make puppets from socks or paper bags?

Did you have pretend tea parties or make mud pies?

Did you draw with sidewalk chalk or finger paints?

What did you make with modeling clay or playdough?

Did you decorate cookies or cupcakes?

Did you invent machines and crazy Lego creatures?

Did you roleplay battles with other neighbor kids?

Did you create food puzzles for your pets?

Did you make up new rules for board or card games?

Do you play with words or write jokes?

Did you dress up and pretend to be someone else?

Now, think about who else was involved. My best creative partner was my little brother, but there were other creative partners, including my pets and stuffed animals.

Who was in your supporting cast at different ages?

_____

_____

_____

Was there someone in your life who discouraged your creativity? Perhaps you were told, "Get your head out of the clouds" or "Stop being silly." When you picture those moments, what do you want to say to that other person?

How would you defend your creative self?

_____

_____

_____

Consider what might be fun now. Don't give the "correct" adult answer. Think about what would <u>really</u> feel fun. For example, I stopped at a craft tent to make a paper kite at the DC Cherry Blossom Festival. Another day, I spent a dollar on a little tub of playdough, and now I play with it almost every week. It's amazing how happy I feel when I let myself play.

What fun toys or opportunities are around you? Can you give yourself permission to stop and play?

_____

_____

_____

God is creative, and if you think he has no fun creating, look at the platypus. What a bizarre, funny little creature. It is so unique that there's nothing else entirely like it. It is part of a small subclass of mammals called monotremes. Within that subclass, the platypus still stands apart from the other four species because it is an aquatic animal. I wonder if God started with the platypus and branched out. Or maybe he just wanted to pique our curiosity about the existence of an animal that has no peers. I think God is like that — that He purposely puts things in our paths to jolt us out of our pattern-making tendencies. We find comfort in patterns. But, when we get too comfortable, we forget about God and lose our connection to his creative spark. Comfort also tends to distance us from God's creative flow.

Name at least one thing you can do today, this week, this month that is both creative and a bit uncomfortable.

_____

_____

_____

Once you let yourself do one fun thing, you may feel inspired to do other creative things. Maybe you will remember a hobby you left behind when you got busy in grad school, or perhaps you will pick up that musical instrument you haven't touched since high school.

If you are having trouble accessing your creativity, consider doing something active to experience the world differently. Do you remember how it felt when you first learned to ride a skateboard or stand on water skis? Or the feeling of freedom while riding a bike with the wind in your face and the joy of weaving back and forth while maintaining your balance? Perhaps your creative spark will emerge when you ride a bike to explore the outdoors instead of forcing yourself to "go exercise."

Like many things in life, the more you tune into the Holy Spirit's creative energy, the easier it becomes, and the more you practice for yourself, the more you have to give to others from a relaxed, confident, and peaceful place. In the Message translation of the Bible, Matthew 11:28-30 reads, "Are you tired? Worn out? Burned out on religion? Come to me. Get away with me, and you'll recover your life. I'll show you how to take a real rest. Walk with me and work with me—watch how I do it. Learn the unforced rhythms of grace. I won't lay anything heavy or ill-fitting on you. Keep company with me, and you'll learn to live freely and lightly." This unforced rhythm of grace can empower your work and personal healing journey and bring you joy.

HELP FOR THERAPISTS

One of the best gifts we can give our clients is offering our valuable skills and knowledge without fear of the client's rejection. Being prepared for questions can help you maintain a calm confidence when presenting EMDR or any other therapeutic options to the client.

Addressing your own fears and doubts

Use the table on the next page to explore your fears about why EMDR won't/can't help. Then brainstorm partial solutions and alternate possibilities.

Issue	Why I think EMDR won't help	How EMDR might help
Bereave-ment	There's no shortcut for grief	Less intense sadness/guilt Access positive memories/ hope
OCD	The client's need for certain-ty cannot be satisfied and may undermine the EMDR process.	Increase access to reali-ty-checking techniques, increase tolerance for uncer-tainty

Preparing your responses

The list below outlines some key points about EMDR therapy.

1. EMDR therapy accesses memory fragments, emotions, and body sensations not associated with words, so it can clear memories that "talk therapy" simply can't reach.
2. EMDR therapy helps calm your body so you can think about a topic or memory without being overwhelmed with emotion.
3. EMDR therapy increases access to positive coping skills and creates exit points out of negative thought spirals and behavioral patterns.
4. EMDR therapy helps shift your creativity from fear-focused to success-focused; it draws on positive experiences and imagery to help you handle future situations well.
5. EMDR therapy helps your brain organize and make sense of distressing memories so you are less likely to have flashbacks, nightmares, and intense emotional responses.
6. EMDR therapy is collaborative. The client decides what topics or memories to address. Nothing is being "done to" the client, the client can pause or stop the desensitization process at any time.

Keeping these ideas in mind, write your answers to the questions in the next table.

Client question	Therapist answer
What is EMDR? How does it work?	
Is EMDR better than talk therapy?	
I've had a lot of bad experiences; will I need to do EMDR therapy forever?	
Can I still talk about things if we do EMDR?	
Do I have to come to the office to do EMDR?	
What if EMDR makes me feel worse?	
Is EMDR like hypnosis?	
How do you do Christian EMDR therapy?	

How can EMDR help someone who:

Grew up in an abusive household?	
Lost a parent?	
Never had any-thing bad happen?	
Had a good childhood but got into an abusive relationship?	
Has experienced a bunch of similar events?	

Are there other questions you feel nervous about answering? Add them to this table. If you feel stuck, consider working with a therapist coach to develop concise answers, address your fearful thoughts, and build your confidence.

Making sense of confusing cases

As I mentioned earlier in the book, Ricky Greenwald's fairy-tale technique for case conceptualization can be a great way to think creatively about a client's story. Here is the format with prompts to help you write the story.

Once upon a time, there was a (insert description of the client's basic identifying features)	
Life was (list out the core emotions and aspects of lifestyle, relationships, etc, before the problem event)	
But one day the dragon came (insert terrible event)	
He/She felt (insert emotional response)	
And believed (insert the negative beliefs)	

These thoughts and feelings get stirred up when (insert triggers)	
To protect himself/ herself, (insert the behavior adaptations)	
This has caused new problems because (insert why the adaptations aren't working)	

Reflections:
What did you learn?

Are you missing any information about the client's situation?

What new paths forward did this creative process unlock?

Finding EMDR targets

Remember that EMDR can target specific memories as well as problematic patterns in thoughts, feelings, and behaviors. Use the questions below to identify the client's problematic beliefs, patterns, and memories.

What does the client care about but fear losing?

What disappointments, betrayals, abandonments, and failures still cause distress for the client?

What problematic relational patterns exist in the client's history?

Is there a mismatch between the client's current identity and who they think they should be?

What are the client's fears about failure? Are there memories of failure that reinforce that fear?

What thoughts or experiences inhibit the client's trust in God?

What thoughts or experiences feed the client's need to control themselves, their circumstances, or the people around them?

Getting into desensitization

Do a "test" before starting memory desensitization. Let the client try different BLS methods (the lightbar, pulsators, drumbeats, tapping on shoulders, tapping on knees). If you have an adjustable system, consider letting the client choose light color, pulsator intensity, speed of the BLS, etc.

Inform clients that everything is adjustable. If something is not working after the first couple of sets, try something different.

Normalize the challenge of holding a visual image in mind during BLS. Although the standard protocol instructs people to watch the image during the BLS sets, it is not strictly necessary.

If the client gets pulled into reliving the memory, shorten the BLS duration and/or increase the speed or intensity of the BLS in order to create more distraction.

If the client struggles to get into the memory, let the client access the thoughts, feelings, and body sensations before starting the BLS set.

If the client seems slow to access and move through memories, consider increasing the duration of BLS.

If the client can't keep the image in mind, give the client permission to notice their thoughts, feelings, and body sensations instead of trying to hold the image.

If the client's mind wanders

If the client's mind is wandering to related memories, keep going.

If the client's mind returns more than once to another specific memory, target that separate memory for a few sets and then return to the original target.

If the client's mind goes to multiple unrelated memories or tasks during the first few BLS sets, explore whether there is any fear about facing the memory.

Explore blocking beliefs. Will resolving the current target cause another problem in the client's life?

If the client can stay with the memory momentarily but consistently ends up somewhere else, consider reducing the duration of BLS to help the client stay focused.

After each BLS set, ask the client to report thoughts, feelings, or body sensations related to the target memory.

If there is no change in thoughts, feelings, or body sensations after several sets, ask where the client's mind goes.

If the client's mind goes blank, instruct the client to focus only on emotions and/or body sensations for a set. If the client is able to stay focused on emotion and body sensation, continue in that manner. Check in on the target memory after several BLS sets.

If the client's mind continues to go blank and the intensity of emotion and body sensations does not change, explore internal resistance and blocking beliefs.

8 Phases of EMDR

1. **History taking** – therapist learns client's story, distressing thoughts, memories, and sensations.

2. **Preparation** – therapist prepares client for challenging emotional work.

3. **Assessment** – client reports images, thoughts, feelings, and body sensations related to a troubling memory.

4. **Desensitization** – therapist guides client in eye-movements or bilateral stimulation (BLS) to reduce intensity of the memory.

5. **Installation** – client associates helpful thoughts to the desensitized memory during BLS.

6. **Body Scan** – client reports on any residual body tension related to the memory; desensitization of body sensations (step 4) is done if needed.

7. **Closure** – therapist assists client in preparing to return to daily life, mentally "putting away" any remaining distress until the next session.

8. **Reassessment** – at the next meeting, client reports on any remaining distress related to the memory.

Stages of Change

1. **Precontemplation** – *Problem? What problem?*

2. **Contemplation** – *Okay, there's a problem.*

3. **Preparation** – *I want to fix the problem.*

4. **Action** – *I'm fixing this problem.*

5. **Maintainance** – *The fix is working.*

SUGGESTED RESOURCES

BOOKS

Brown, J. and Errington, L. (2019). Introduction. Brown, J. and Errington, L. (Eds). *Bowen family systems theory in Christian ministry: Grappling with Theory and its Application through a Biblical Lens.* (pp. 1-18). The Family Systems Practice. https://www.thefsi.com.au/wp-content/uploads/2023/04/Bowen-family-systems-theory-in-Christian-ministry.pdf

Keyes, B. (2023). *The Heart Model: An Integrated Faith-based and Psychological Approach to Heal from Trauma and Produce Balance in the Mind, Body, and Spirit.* Renown Publishing.

Parnell, L. (2013). *Attachment-Focused EMDR: Healing Relational Trauma.* W. W. Norton & Company.

Shapiro, F. (2017). *Eye Movement Desensitization and Reprocessing (EMDR) Therapy: Basic Principles, Protocols, and Procedures.* (3rd Ed.). The Guilford Press.

Shapiro, F. (2012). *Getting Past Your Past: Take Control of Your Life With Self-Help Techniques from EMDR Therapy.* Rodale Books.

Van der Kolk, Bessel. (2014). *The Body Keeps the Score: Brain, Mind, and Body in the Healing of Trauma.* Penguin Books.

ARTICLES

Development of Expert Networks: A Hybrid System of Expert Systems and Neural Networks. (retrieved May 3, 2025). https://www.sciencedirect.com/topics/engineering/left-hemisphere

Falkenstein, Tom. "What Being Highly Sensitive Really Means." *Psychology Today.* December 10, 2019. https://www.psychologytoday.com/us/blog/the-highly-sensitive-man/201912/what-being-highly-sensitive-really-means

Keely, B. L. "Is the Human Brain a Prediction Machine?" *Reason Magazine.* March 2024. (retrieved

May 16, 2025). https://reason.com/2024/02/20/creating-our-own-simulations/

Keers, R. et al., "A genome-wide test of the differential susceptibility hypothesis reveals a genetic predictor of differential response to psychological treatments for child anxiety disorders." *Psychotherapy and Psychosomatics*. 2016.

BLOGPOSTS

Greenwald, Ricky. "The Fairy Tale: A Model for Post-Traumatic Growth." Trauma Institute & Child Trauma Institute. March 27, 2015. https://www.ticti.org/fairy-tale/

Whitaker, L. E. (2018, May 3). How Does Thinking Positive Thoughts Affect Neuroplasticity? https://meteoreducation.com/how-does-thinking-positive-thoughts-affect-neuroplasticity/

WEBSITES

Consciousness studies:
 https://www.sussex.ac.uk/research/centres/sussex-centre-for-consciousness-science/publications

Highly Sensitive Persons:
http://www.tomfalkenstein.com/therapy.html
https://hsperson.com/

GLOSSARY

Action stage The fourth stage of change, when a person is actively implementing changes in thoughts and behaviors.

Adaptive Information Processing Model (AIP) The theory that the human brain selects information from experiences to develop and revise frameworks about how the world functions, how to make sense of sensory input, and how the person should respond to different situations.

Attachment-Focused EMDR (AF-EMDR) A relatively new branch of EMDR developed by Dr. Laurel Parnell.

Attention-Deficit and Hyperactivity Disorder (ADHD) A mental health disorder described in the Diagnostic and Statistics Manual (DSM). There are multiple presentations of this disorder including people who have trouble staying still and people who are easily distracted or have difficulty figuring out what information is important versus what is best ignored. Other symptoms include difficulty keeping things in step or chronological order, difficulty estimating time or realizing how much time has past, and difficulty completing tasks. Some individuals demonstrate a tendency to hyper-focus, over-plan and engage in controlling behaviors.

Basic Training The teaching and consultation process designed to provide a minimum level of competence in EMDR therapy.

Bilateral stimulation (BLS) Movement or stimulation that alternates from one side of the body to the other. Examples include eye-movements, tapping, sounds that originate from alternating sides.

Case Conceptualization The process of theorizing why a client's problems exist and persist as well as what could help the client reach their desired goals.

Continuing Education Unit (CEU) Ongoing education that mental health professionals are required to complete in order to maintain professional competence. These credits are accumulated through a variety of learning opportunities including workshops, seminars, conferences, college courses, supervision, etc.

Christian, A Disciple of Jesus Christ A person who believes the "Gospel" or "good news," that if we believe that **Jesus** is the son of **God**, believe that he died and came back to life, and accept that He paid the death penalty for all our willful and ignorant errors against God and others, then we will be saved from death and despair. We have another life after we die and it will be a life of joy, peace, and safety. In the meantime, we have the **Holy Spirit** who guides us, providing us with God's wisdom and knowledge, far beyond what our five senses tell us and giving us hope even when circumstances seem hopeless. To obtain this gift we do nothing except agree to follow Him, sacrificing our unhealthy desires, urges, impulses, and desires for control. We find peace in knowing that God has good plans for us and He is the one who ultimately opens or closes the doors of opportunity.

Contemplation stage The second stage of change in which a person starts to recognize a problem and the potential need for change.

Dual-Awareness Stimulation (DAS) The process of observing a memory while noticing the current surroundings. This phrase is sometimes used instead of BLS.

Emotional Freedom Technique (EFT) A therapeutic intervention that involves tapping on meridian points on the body.

Eye-Movement Desensitization and Reprocessing (EMDR) A therapy model that includes BLS as an intervention. See Appendix for Quick reference of phases or Chapter 4 for more detailed overview.

EMDR Global Network An organization that offers certification to validate the competence of EMDR clinicians. It provides a broader definition of basic training and thus is more inclusive of EMDR training models used outside of the United States.

EMDR International Association (EMDRIA) An organization that credentials EMDR therapists. EMDRIA was the first credentialing organization, but others now exist both in the US and around the world.

Future Template A technique in EMDR that encourages a client to imagine handling a future scenario in a way that is calm, confident, and effective.

Homeostatis The way a biological system maintains stability while adjusting to change. This can apply to the physical and emotional aspects within a person as well as the interpersonal dynamics between pairs or groups of people.

Highly Sensitive Person (HSP) An term an individual might use to describe their information processing difficulties. HSPs tend to be easily overwhelmed with there is too much sensory information in the environment. See Suggested Resources for resources about this topic.

Internal Family Systems (IFS) A model of therapy that works with the different parts or aspects of a person to help resolve the client's internal conflicts.

Negative cognition (NC) A negative belief the client has about themselves as it relates to a troubling memory.

Maintenance stage The fifth stage of change, when a person has completed planned changes and developed new habits.

Positive cognition (PC) A positive belief the client would like to believe about themselves when they think about a particular memory.

Precontemplation stage The first stage of change, when a person does not acknowledge that there is a problem or need for change.

Post-Traumatic Stress Disorder (PTSD) A mental health disorder described in the Diagnostic and Statistics Manual. The disorder is characterized by experiencing or witnessing a life-threatening (or preceived life threatening situation) and developing recurring thoughts, body sensations, nightmares, and heightened reactions to similar events or reminders of the memory. PTSD symptoms can also include avoidance of reminders, hyper-vigilance, mood instability, etc.

Stages of Change A behavioral therapy framework outlining five stages that indicate a person's readiness to make a change. See Stages of Change graphic on page 174.

Sensory Processing Sensitivity (SPS) A condition that makes it difficult for an individual to separate themselves or "tune out" external stimuli. A person with this disorder may refer to themself as highly-sensitive persons (HSP).

Subjective Unit of Disturbance (SUD) A rating of how intense emotions and body sensations are at a particular moment. This is one step in the EMDR assessment process.

Target or Target Memory The memory, series of experiences, repetitive thoughts, or body sensations used as the focus during the EMDR desensitization process.

Transtheoretical Model (TTM) A behavioral change model that introduced the stages of change framework.

Validity of Cognition (VOC) A rating of the felt truth or accuracy of a positive statement. This rating is one step in the EMDR assessment process.

ABOUT THE AUTHOR

Angela Sarafin is a Licensed Marriage and Family Therapist (LMFT), Licensed Professional Counselor (LPC), Eye Movement, Desensitization and Reprocessing (EMDR) certified therapist, and NeuroGraphica Specialist. She graduated with a Masters of Arts (M.A.) in Behavioral Science - Family Therapy from the University of Houston - Clear Lake in 2007 and completed her counseling practicum at a substance abuse treatment center working with both the individuals and families. She continued her post-graduate work in an early-intervention program for at-risk youth, serving as both counselor and program director. After leaving the non-profit world she opened a private practice in Houston, TX in 2011 where she offered faith-based counseling and mentoring. She started a second practice after her husband's job relocated them to Washington, DC in 2015. She particularly enjoys working with clients who are seeking recovery from trauma, dealing with women's issues and individuals seeking clarity in life. Her unique way of providing creative, faith-based trauma therapy has facilitated healing and spiritual development for many clients over the years.

Her cat Cactipuss oversaw all aspects of this publication.

www.ingramcontent.com/pod-product-compliance
Lightning Source LLC
Chambersburg PA
CBHW070109030426
42335CB00016B/2076